BONSAI
in Your Home

An Indoor Grower's Guide

Paul Lesniewicz

Sterling Publishing Co., Inc.
New York

Library of Congress Cataloging-in-Publication Data

Lesniewicz, Paul.
   [Bonsai im Haus. English]
   Bonsai in your home : an indoor grower's guide / by Paul
Lesniewicz.
      p.   cm.
   Includes index.
   ISBN 0-8069-0780-0
   1. Indoor bonsai.   I. Title.
SB433.5.L45513   1994
635.9'772—dc20   94-17466
                                                      CIP

10   9   8   7   6   5   4   3   2   1

First paperback edition published in 1996 by
Sterling Publishing Company, Inc.
387 Park Avenue South, New York, N.Y. 10016
Originally published in Germany and © 1991 by
Verlag BCH, Bonsai-Centrum Heidelberg
under the title *Bonsai im Haus*
English translation © 1994 by Sterling Publishing Co., Inc.
Distributed in Canada by Sterling Publishing
% Canadian Manda Group, One Atlantic Avenue, Suite 105
Toronto, Ontario, Canada M6K 3E7
Distributed in Great Britain and Europe by Cassell PLC
Wellington House, 125 Strand, London WC2R 0BB, England
Distributed in Australia by Capricorn Link (Australia) Pty Ltd.
P.O. Box 6651, Baulkham Hills, Business Centre, NSW 2153, Australia
Printed and bound in China
All rights reserved

Sterling ISBN 0-8069-0780-0 Trade
            0-8069-0781-9 Paper

Photo on title page: *Portulacaria afra.*

English translation by Elizabeth Reinersmann

The editor thanks Mr. F. Chase Rosade of Rosade Bonsai Studio, New
Hope, Pennsylvania, for his advice in the preparation of the English
edition.

BONSAI
in Your Home

CONTENTS

Starting from the Beginning . . .
Propagating Your Own Indoor Bonsai

Starting bonsai from seed, cuttings, or plants you have collected is not all that difficult. All you need, after studying this chapter, is a little patience, imagination, and luck

Miniature Bonsai
The Smallest of the Small Are Becoming Popular

They are 6 inches (15 cm) tall at most. The containers used for growing them fit easily in the palm of a child's hand. This chapter describes their needs and how to care for them

The Most Beautiful Indoor Bonsai from Around the World
Origin, Location, Care, and Shaping

As if it were a beautiful picture book, you will turn to this section time and again, but it is also a reference. You can consult it for essential information about any one of the 42 favorite bonsai plants arranged alphabetically. Symbols inform you at a glance about each plant's essential temperature, light, and water requirements, and the text explains location, watering, transplanting, soil, wiring, pruning, and propagation. Additional plants for indoor bonsai are listed at the end of the section

Answers to Important Questions
Good Advice from Bonsai Specialists

How often should shoots be cut back? What is a solitaire? How important is the age of a bonsai plant in determining its value? Concise answers are given to frequently asked questions

Buying Indoor Bonsai
How to Avoid Paying for Mistakes

Here you will learn what characteristics make a bonsai high-quality, according to experts. You will learn what to look for when buying a plant

Index

Alphabetical listing of plant names (Latin names and common names) and other information

Growth, Development, Understanding . . .

Chinese landscape.

Loving Bonsai and the Art of Losing Oneself

The purpose of this book is to instruct as well as stimulate. It is intended as a helping hand for garden hobbyists and plant lovers so that they can become successful in cultivating small indoor trees. However, it can also serve as a means for those that are not close to nature to find an escape from the turmoil of life to more harmony and calmness.

Far Eastern traditions—including the art of creating bonsai—are appealing to more and more people in the West. All of these traditions—archery, flower arranging, and landscape painting—are rooted in Zen Buddhism. They are considered "artless arts," meaning that mastering an art consists of going beyond the mere practice of techniques, instead centering one's own involvement on the process.

Those who take up the creation of bonsai and stay with it over a period of time will gain self-awareness, experience time, and in the process gain a sense of happiness.

Bonsai shrubs and trees that thrive indoors have special meaning for Westerners. Since very early in our history, home has been a place where we felt secure, a place we created and managed; it was part of our identity. From antiquity on, Europeans brought nature into their homes; growing potted plants indoors is part of our domestic tradition. It is only natural, therefore, that the Far Eastern art of cultivating small trees in containers—the art of bonsai—has been adopted in the West.

Plants suitable for growing indoors as bonsai often have symbolic meanings, which inspire us, however subconsciously, while we shape and care for them. The myrtle has been a symbol of joy for centuries; the olive tree is a symbol of wisdom and dignity. Tending bonsai plants is a way to rediscover the laws of nature and to further understand their meaning. To observe and cultivate these small but strong and often gnarled plants over many years will train our eyes, sharpen our senses, and sometimes allow us to forget ourselves.

From the works of Martinus Opifex (1440), Lovers with Plants on a Table.

Indoor Bonsai: Nature or Culture?

On the ninth day I will return and continue enjoying the chrysanthemums.

—Mong Hao-Jan

Top: Mural painting in the tomb of Prince Zhang Huai from the Tang Dynasty.
Bottom: In Chinese families, the art of creating bonsai is handed down from generation to generation.

The History of Small Trees for the Home

The art of *penjing*, or miniature landscapes, has been part of Chinese culture since the Tang dynasty (618–906). Its beauty has been passed on in poems and paintings, usually reserved for the noble and the rich. In addition to Zen, the close relationship that existed between people and nature during that time greatly influenced the creation of bonsai. A reverence for simple forms, a sense of the essential, and attention to the harmony found in nature are the basic foundations of bonsai culture—and have remained so to this day.

In China, and later also in Japan, the goal was to capture trees in their full beauty and grace and to recreate them as bonsai plants that would be as similar to their big brothers as possible.

At this point, let us, once and for all, clear up a common misconception of Westerners: that the shapes and forms of miniature trees are due to genetic alteration. That is not true. Time and again, careful observation will reveal that the flowers and fruit of a miniature tree are not significantly smaller than those of a large tree. This means that only the trunk of the tree and its branches are kept small by the skillful tending of the bonsai gardener—something that also takes place in nature because of the influence of climate. The genetic structure of the plant remains unaltered.

In China, a bonsai is considered a precious heirloom and is handed down from one generation to another, just as gardening know-how is passed on from father to son to make sure that the art of bonsai will never be forgotten.

Towards the end of the Ming dynasty (1368–1644), Buddhist monks (or, according to another legend, a Chinese official) brought bonsai culture to Japan. Like so many other art forms from China, the art of creating bonsai reached new heights in Japan. To this day, Japanese gardeners cultivate small bonsai of unsurpassed beauty and clarity of form. And it was in Japan where the name *bon-sai*, meaning "tree in a tray," was coined. From Japan, this art form began to spread

In the Shinto religion, trees are worshipped as gods.

through Europe, however slowly; enthusiasm for and mastery of the art really became widespread only in the last few centuries.

Until the 1970s, these small bonsai trees were grown only outdoors, just like their big brothers. In Europe we kept them on balconies, terraces, and patios, and in the garden. It is understandable that indoor bonsai—those living inside the house—developed in the Western world, since Westerners generally live more indoors than outdoors. People living in large, modern cities were fascinated with the idea of bringing these small trees and bushes indoors. Formerly they could only be seen from a window or only spend a few hours inside our house, like guests. People longed to be closer to nature and house plants weren't enough anymore. We are sure that the development of indoor bonsai was also inspired by Western myths about trees: with these small trees, people brought the symbol of strength and life into their homes.

How can we understand these trees that grow and thrive inside our homes? They are plants whose life rhythms do not depend on the change of seasons and whose natural climate is similar to that inside our homes. Tropical and subtropical trees and shrubs fulfill these requirements. In their places of origin, temperature and seasonal changes are minimal; vegetation there depends to a very minimal degree on a dormant period, unlike the plants that remain outside in temperate regions in the winter. Particularly in tropical forests, where the climate is warm and humid, a vast number of plants and trees live for hundreds of years. It is from these regions that we find the many species suitable for our wonderful indoor bonsai: rubber trees, bamboo, Schefflera, jacaranda, and many others. Gardenia, azalea, citrus trees, camellia, pomegranate, myrtle, olive, and pine trees, and many other beautiful and very interesting plants, come to us from the subtropical Mediterranean region. All of these plants can be used to create indoor bonsai; of course, they can also be grown outdoors.

Understanding these plants and knowing how to transplant them safely and according to their natural requirements is essential for growing indoor bonsai. Every plant lover and friend of bonsai is aware that in the natural world trees and bushes live outside, so plants kept inside the home need a rest period from time to time in the garden or on the balcony. Of course, in many climates, such "vacations" can only be scheduled during the summer, which is the time that the temperate climate most closely resembles the plants' original habitat.

Top: The legendary 1000-year-old banyan tree at Lijiang River in China.

*An old olive tree
growing in the Mediterranean
region.*

What You Need to Know About Location and Care

Some people talk to their plants; I believe it is more important that I listen to them.

—Dan Barton

Bonsai Gardeners Share Their Experiences

Seldom will we get simple answers when asking for advice from someone who truly is an "old hand," because every plant is different. However, the location and care of an indoor bonsai are determined by the climate that exists in its native habitat. Because that climate determines its needs, tolerances, and sensitivity to the environment, one of the most important facts, therefore, is to know where an indoor bonsai originally came from.

What bonsai growers will become aware of over time is the interaction of the different components of the environment. For instance, the more light your bonsai receives, the higher the room temperature can be; the higher the temperature, the more water a plant needs . . . and so forth. With the advice and suggestions you find in this book, combined with the knowledge you gain from your own experience, you too will become a master.

Light

Like people, plants cannot live without light. If we lived only in darkness, all of us would get sick, because only light can transform air, water, and nutrition into growth and life. When selecting places for your indoor bonsai, don't forget that in almost all cases the summer and winter months are equally long, and the light during the day is more intense in the plants' native habitat than it is in temperate zones. Also, remember that most homes have only a few places—particularly during the winter months—where the amount of daylight available to plants is sufficient. The ideal spot would be a place by the window where light is not obstructed by large trees, high walls, or a roof overhang. Even 3 feet (1 m) away from a window, the degree of luminosity is greatly diminished, although this is not noticed by our eyes. That might already be too dark for a bonsai. If that is the case, you will notice that your bonsai becomes straggly and tall. If you notice that your plant doesn't seem to receive sufficient light on one side, turn it around once a month.

Various bonsai trees, arranged on trays before a window, with an additional light source.

Luxometer.

Light means sunlight, but—particularly during the height of the summer season—not direct exposure to sun. Especially during the middle of the day, this might be too much for even the most sun-hungry plant. Protect plants by adjusting window blinds, or use a light-transmitting shade. The minimum amount of light your bonsai needs is listed in the table on pages 13 and 14. The degree of brightness is measured with a luxometer—a very simple and inexpensive instrument that is similar to the light meter used for taking photographs. Artificial light is needed if the lux level in your bonsai place is below that given in the table. The more artificial light your plants needs, the longer the artificial lights need to be on—perhaps from 12 to 16 hours. Accuracy in terms of the length of time artificial lights are on is very important for your plant. You need to turn them on and off at the same times each day. This can easily be accomplished with the help of a timer.

Providing sufficient light is a particular problem during the winter months in temperate regions, even if the plant is kept on a windowsill. The days are simply too short. Lengthen those days with the help of artificial light: in the morning before sunrise and in the evening after sundown. During October and March, you might need approximately one hour; during November and February, two hours; and during December and January, about three hours. This will vary depending on where you live. Here, too, a timer is very helpful.

Regular incandescent light bulbs are not suitable light sources. Their light does not correspond to that provided by normal daylight; your plants may even suffer damage from the excessive heat that they produce.

Glass shelves with additional light sources.

It's best to use artificial light that approximates sunlight in giving a wide spectrum of colors of light. Choose fluorescent lights that have daylight and warm light ranges. This gives a better result than plant lights that are in the violet range only. Fluorescent lights, like those used to provide light for fish tanks, are good sources of artificial light. Depending on the light source used, your lights, generally speaking, should be suspended about 10 to 32 inches (25 to 81 cm) above the plants.

As your bonsai collection grows—and if you start to run out of space—you might find glass shelves to be very effective. They make optimal use of available daylight as well as the artificial light that you are supplying. Since the amount of the light is inversely proportional to the square of the distance between the plant and the light source, shorten the distance for those plants that are particularly "light-hungry."

Bonsai Plants and Their Light Requirements

Plant	Lux Requirement
Adenium obesum	1000
Aralia sieboldii	1000
Araucaria heterophylla	800
Ardisia crenata	1000
Aucuba japonica	800
Azalea	1000
Bougainvillea glabra	2000
Buxus harlandii	800
Cactaceae	2000
Calliandra brevipes	2000
Camellia japonica	1000
Carmona microphylla	1000
Casuarina equisetifolia	1500
Chamaecyparis	1000
Chamaedorea	800
Cissus rhombifolia	800
Citrus microcarpa	2000
Cocos nucifera	1000
Coffea arabica	1500
Cotoneaster	1500
Crassula arborescens	1000
Cupressus macrocarpa	1000
Cycas	800
Eugenia	1500
Euphorbia balsamifera	2000

To convert lux to footcandles, the unit of illumination more common in the U.S., multiply by 0.4. One lux = 1 lumen/square meter. One footcandle = 1 lumen/square foot.

Plant	Lux Requirement
Euphorbia pulcherrima	2000
Fatshedera	800
Ficus benjamina	1000
Ficus benjamina 'Lucy,' 'Natascha'	1000
Ficus buxifolia	2000
Ficus virens	2000
Ficus carica	1500
Ficus neriifolia	2000
Ficus panda	800
Ficus pumila	1000
Ficus religiosa, F. virens	2000
Ficus retusa, F. natalensis	1000
Ficus rubiginosa	1000
Fortunella hindsii	2000
Fuchsia	800
Gardenia jasminoides	1000
Grevillea robusta	1500
Hedera helix	1000
Helxinia	1000
Hibiscus	1500
Holarrhena	2000
Jacaranda mimosifolia	1500
Jacobinia carnea	1000
Lagerstroemia indica	2000
Lantana camara	2000
Ligustrum	1000
Lonicera nitida	800
Malpighia coccigera	1500
Murraya paniculata	1000
Myricaria cauliflora	1500
Myrtus communis	1000
Olea europaea	1000
Passiflora carnea	1000
Pellionia repens	800
Pistacia vera	1000
Pittosporum tobira	500
Podocarpus macrophyllus	800
Poinsettia	1500
Polyscias fruticosa	1500
Portulacaria afra	1000
Psidium guajava	2000
Punica granatum	1500
Pyracantha	1000
Rosmarinus officinalis	1000
Sageretia theezans	1000
Samanea saman	2000
Schefflera actinophylla	800
Selaginella	1000
Serissa foetida	1000
Tamarindus	2000
Ulmus parvifolia	1000

Triphasia trifolia.

Air and Humidity

Fresh air and sufficient humidity are as important for small trees as they are for all other plants, as well as for people and for furniture made from wood. This presents no problem during the summer; plants can be brought outside, to a terrace, a balcony, or the garden. Just make sure that they have a chance to adjust slowly to the light, air, and sun. The best way is to bring them out in small steps. Start with a few hours on somewhat cloudy days in early spring when the sun has not yet reached the intensity it has in the summer. Bonsai lovers in Heidelberg, Germany, came up with the idea of an outside windowsill—simple and ingenious. Plants can be placed outside or inside, depending on the weather.

During the winter months when we turn on the heating system, our small trees need some help: 40% to 50% humidity is ideal. If you don't like electric humidifiers (which, of course, are the most reliable), put pottery trays filled with water near the plants and on top of the heat registers. Either way, this is also very beneficial for human respiratory passages.

Another possibility for providing the necessary humidity is to place your bonsai plant on a tray filled with sand or gravel. Keep the sand or gravel damp at all times. Such a setup works well for plants on a windowsill that has a radiator or heat register underneath.

You'll find some special and very decorative suggestions in the section on "Picturesque Indoor Bonsai for a Healthier Indoor Environment"; see page 71.

Humid air is very important for your bonsai because it reduces water loss by transpiration, by which a plant might lose more water than it is able to take up through its roots if the air is too dry. If the plant loses too much water, stomates, located on the underside of the leaves, close up; the exchange of gases necessary for photosynthesis is interrupted; and the growing process is disturbed. Something similar happens when the stomates are clogged by dust. That is why we recommend giving your plants a gentle shower in the bathtub once a month.

Keep in mind, when buying a bonsai, that your house may be particularly dry in winter and perhaps somewhat dusty—depending on the type and the amount of heat and the type of insulation—so choose accordingly. Some bonsai plants are more sensitive than others to dry conditions; those with thick, somewhat leathery leaves lose moisture less easily and are more suitable to conditions where

*Top: An outside windowsill—one possibility when you have no access to a garden or a balcony.
Bottom: Bonsai placed on a tray filled with sand or gravel.*

Ficus benjamina, with roots over a rock.

the humidity is low. A good example is the *Ficus buxifolia*. Its large, soft leaves are a sign that a great deal of transpiration takes place; such a plant needs a high degree of humidity. *Lantana* is another example. For this reason, anyone who has indoor plants should also have a hygrometer.

Another factor to keep in mind in many regions during the winter months is drafts. Tropical plants are particularly sensitive to them. The lower the outside temperature, the more risky it is to open the window—even for just a moment. If it is very cold outside, bonsai gardeners recommend removing plants from the windowsill before opening the window. For those of you who can't take your bonsai outside in summer, we give the following advice: during the summer months, air out your house often.

Temperature

When you think about the requirements necessary for your bonsai, remember that no plant was created for indoor living. The climate in the plant's native habitat must be your guide for creating a suitable environment indoors. This is particularly important when it comes to temperature. Depending on where you want to create your "green island" in your home, choose bonsai that are subtropical (coldhouse) or tropical (heated greenhouse).

Subtropical trees and bushes are accustomed to warm summers and cool winters in their natural habitat. When outside, they like to be in an area that is protected from the wind (get them used to the outdoors slowly). Indoors, during the winter months, they like cool locations, ideally, with temperatures from 41° to 59°F (5° to 15°C) during the day and somewhat lower during the night. A smart and sensible bonsai gardener will place subtropical bonsai on a balcony or terrace, or in the bedroom or hallway, or the staircase, all depending on the time of year.

Bonsai in a winter garden.

Tropical plants should be kept warm throughout the year, because in their natural habitat they grow almost without a dormant period. They are most comfortable with daytime temperatures from 64° to 75°F (18° to 24°C), and 57°F (14°C) to 61°F (16°C) at night, the normal temperature ranges in many modern homes during the winter. Tropical bonsai, therefore, can be placed directly over a heating source during the winter without losing too much moisture if the proper air humidity is provided. What your tropical bonsai do *not* like are "cold feet," which happens when the area around the roots is colder than the surrounding air. This can occur if you have a stone or a marble windowsill or when cold air penetrates through small cracks.

Specific temperatures and other care instructions for some of the most beautiful, special, and most favorite indoor bonsai can be found in the second part of this book. It is best to look there before you decide on a particular plant, or when you are choosing the most appropriate location for your bonsai.

Watering

In China, the homeland of so many different bonsai, the frequency of watering depends on the prevailing temperature.

Too much is as bad as too little. For this reason, containers used for bonsai plants have large drainage holes in the bottom. A proper soil mixture ensures that the soil surrounding the roots does not hold too much water.

While we are on the subject of "too much," it is also important to mention what is called "wet feet." They are extremely unhealthy for bonsai plants and occur when the bottom of the tray or saucer on which the container is placed has not been filled with either sand or gravel. Water left in a tray or saucer can cause root rot. Therefore, remember to remove excess water from the tray.

Bonsai plants, when compared to other potted plants, react very poorly when the soil becomes dry. This can easily happen, since the roots of a bonsai plant characteristically have very little space.

How often, then, should you water your plants? This depends to a great extent on the species of plant, its location, and the time of year. And what about "the how" of watering? The rule of thumb is this: slowly and with water that is at room temperature. Furthermore, our rainwater is not what it used to be. Therefore, we recommend letting the tapwater stand at room temperature for 24 hours before using it for watering. Cold tapwater used immediately will shock the plant, because it suddenly lowers the temperature of the soil and the roots are unable to absorb the water or nutrients.

Hard (calcareous) water over time also changes the chemical composition of the soil. The amount of acid in the soil (measured in pH) diminishes over time. The ideal pH value is 5.5 to 6.5. You can find out the degree of hardness of your tapwater at your local plant nursery or at the water department.

If you detect a whitish deposit around the stem of your plant or on the edge of the container, your water is too hard and it's a clear sign that you need a water softener. You can soften the water by either boiling it or adding a softener. Using a water filter is another possibility. Such water-treatment appliances and supplements are available in specialty stores. Gardeners have also found that mineral water is very effective.

Watering should be done in several stages. Only then can the soil absorb the water properly. If the soil is very dry, it won't be able to absorb the necessary water. The water will run right through it, into the saucer or tray. Be patient; just continue to water and do so very slowly.

Immersing a plant in water, a good way of watering. Top: immerse the plant. Middle: leave it in until all the air bubbles rise. Bottom: remove the plant.

Bonsai should never be allowed to dry out completely. The bonsai gardeners will see, hear, and feel when their plants need to be watered. For instance, it is high time to water when you see new shoots becoming limp. Dry soil crumbles between your fingers, feels warmer than when it is moist, and is lighter in color. Also, when you knock against the pot or container and the soil is very dry, you can hear a hollow sound. When you water and you see the water rapidly draining through to the saucer, you know it is time to water. When soaking your plant—immersing the container beyond the rim in a water bath—wait until all the air has been pushed out (you won't see any more air bubbles rising to the surface). By the way, soaking your little tree in a water bath is much more efficient than watering from the top.

The soil of a bonsai plant should always be slightly moist—but never wet. However, if you notice that the soil remains wet for an unusually long time, it might be a sign of a problem in the root system or soil that isn't draining well. Repotting—including root trimming—is probably in order.

Every plant needs a good rain shower from time to time. Plants that are outside during the summer will usually get their fair share of rain, but those that are always inside can benefit greatly from a shower in the bathtub—again, with water at room temperature.

Be careful, however: do not expose plants to direct sunlight while the leaves are still wet. Water drops will act like magnifying glasses. Also, when it is very hot—at midday—water only the soil, or immerse the whole plant in a water bath.

Avoid giving your plant a shower or spraying it with water in the evening. Lower nighttime temperatures may not allow its leaves to dry completely, which can lead to fungus and other diseases.

It's very important for you to be attentive when watering, immersing, or spraying your plants. Every tree is different and goes through different stages during the course of the year. The more you watch your indoor plant, the lower are the chances that you will make a mistake.

By the way, the degree of moisture in the soil can be measured with a simple and inexpensive device—a hygrometer.

A hygrometer, for measuring the amount of water in the soil.

Feeding

The minerals dissolved in water aren't sufficient; plants need nourishment from the soil. Fresh potting soil has all the necessary nutrients, such as nitrogen, phosphorus, potash, lime, sulfur, iron, and trace elements. Since bonsai trees, unlike other plants, grow in very little soil and the available nutrients are quickly used up, adding a liquid fertilizer to the water every four to six weeks is very important.

Organic Fertilizer is made from either plant or animal substances. In order to be available to the plant it must be changed into nutrient salts. With liquid organic fertilizers, like organic liquid bonsai fertilizer, this process has already been completed. If you want to give your bonsai a special treat, add a pulverized organic fertilizer once during the main growing season; this will improve the flora in the soil.

Inorganic or Full-Spectrum Fertilizers, like those normally used for flowers, are also very good for indoor plants. Just make sure that you use less than the amount recommended by the manufacturer. You might follow this rule of thumb: Cut the suggested amount in half and feed more often; during the summer months, approximately every 2 to 4 weeks; during fall and winter, every 6 to 8 weeks. If the place where you keep your plants is not heated and has little light, do not fertilize them during the cold season. Always fertilize when the soil is wet. When the soil is dry, the fertilizer may act too harshly, which could damage the very small roots.

When Feeding, Less Is Often More. Whenever your bonsai looks wilted and wretched and uses up only a little water, do not make the mistake of trying to combat the "crisis" by giving it more food. On the contrary, you should discontinue feeding. Take the plant out of the container and examine the roots. If the ends are brown instead of white and mushy to the touch and the "skin" comes off easily, you will know why the plant looks so sickly: the roots are dead and are unable to absorb nutrition from the soil or from the fertilizer. Should this be the case, cut off all dead roots and transplant your tree into fresh soil. But do not fertilize it until new roots have developed. In addition, do not fertilize your tree just before or when it is in bloom. It will use the additional energy to grow new shoots, and buds and flowers might fall off.

When it comes to fertilizing, there are no generally applicable rules covering all bonsai plants. Here, too, it is important to keep an eye on your plants, taking into consideration where they originally came from, where in your home they now live, and what your own experience has taught you. You need to have enough confidence to trust that experience—a fundamental tenet of bonsai-culture from the Far East.

In the second part of the book (pages 87 to 173) we have compiled a guide for many of the favorite indoor bonsai, which includes specific information about feeding each species.

Do not fertilize when a plant is in bloom.

Diseases and Pests

Plants are much like people; when they feel comfortable in their environment and are well cared for, they tend to get sick less often. Their natural resistance protects them against diseases and pests. But if they are compromised too much as a result of, for example, poor air circulation or temperatures that are too high, or lack of care (which sometimes cannot be avoided), your bonsai might fall prey to fungi or pests. Prevention—meaning attentive and tender care—is the best medicine. However, even the most expertly cared for plants can get sick. For this reason, on the next few pages, we list the most common plant diseases and pests. With this information, you may be able to effectively intervene early. Fortunately for all of us who love nature and plants, it is now easier than ever to combat diseases with organic, biological methods, as natural and environmentally "friendly" products have to a large degree replaced chemical preparations.

Diseases are discussed first. In most cases, their causes can be found and eliminated in the plant's environment. However, the "patient" must also be treated, which relieves the plant from having to invest too much of its own energy in recuperating. When using disease-fighting products, make sure you pay special attention to the instructions provided by the manufacturer. In order to prevent pests from developing resistance to a particular pesticide, it is a good idea to alternate between different preparations.

Powdery Mildew is a fungus infection occurring on the tops of leaves. It usually is the result of too little air circulation, or may result if a plant has been sprayed too late in the evening and the water didn't have a chance to evaporate. True mildew also can be caused by a plant fertilizer too high in nitrogen. If possible, treat your plant with a natural antimildew fungicide.

Downy Mildew is a grey covering on the underside of leaves, with yellow spots on the top. It is caused when air circulation around the plant is insufficient or the humidity in the air and the water content of the soil are too high. To treat a plant with false mildew, relocate the affected plant to a place with better air circulation and spray it with a fungicide—the earlier, the better. A spray of 1 tablespoon (15 mL) sodium bicarbonate plus 2 tablespoons horticultural oil dissolved in 1 quart of water (1000 mL) can be used as a fungicide for either type of mildew. Some plants become photosensitive, however, after being sprayed, so check with a nursery to be sure before using this recipe.

Chlorosis. Your plant has chlorosis when the leaves turn yellow while the veins remain green. This iron deficiency can be eliminated by adding a chelated iron supplement to the water.

Sooty Mold is a black, sootlike deposit that appears primarily on older leaves and often only on one side of the plant. This fungus growth usually follows infestation by aphids (plant lice). The fungus grows on the honeydew the aphids secrete. Treat your plant with a contact insecticide.

Root Rot may result when water remains in the saucer for too long, or when the plant has been fed too heavily. It may cause the leaves to become discolored, or branches may break off. Affected roots and root fibres turn brown and mushy and must be removed. After the affected portion of the roots system has been cut off, transplant the plant with fresh soil and water it well. For the next couple of weeks, reduce watering so that new roots have a chance to grow and are able to take up water. Do not fertilize your plant for the next 8 weeks, at least. Also, during this time of convalescence, do not expose your plant to direct sunlight.

Pests can also be fought successfully with beneficial insects, particularly if the pests are detected early. Using natural predators—

natural enemies of a pest—is often very difficult for gardeners to accept at first. However, once they have observed this natural process of combating pests, most quickly become convinced of its effectiveness.

The basic principle underlying this approach has to do with competition between organisms. By using the natural enemies of a pest, the pest can be kept from multiplying. In the absence of the pests' natural enemies, as is often the case with small trees in containers, the pests can multiply and in the end consume your plant.

When using the beneficial insects, you will note that they only live as long as their food (the pests) is available. When the food is gone, so are the predators.

For this treatment to work, temperatures must be at least 64°F (18°C). You need to also be aware that this method will not work as fast as chemical pesticides. Be patient. Growing bonsai requires patience anyhow. Now let's look at the specific pests.

Aphids are usually found on the underside of leaves or around a newly forming bud. They literally suck the life out of a plant. Often it is sufficient to give the plant a shower (in the bathtub) in order to get rid of them. If this doesn't work, spray the plant with a garden spray containing pyrethrum, like Metasystox. If you want to use the natural predators, you will have success with lacewing larvae, known as "aphid lions." Also, yellow stickers (cards with a sticky surface) are very effective against flying aphids. The yellow color attracts them, and they adhere to the sticky substance.

Scales appear as small, brownish mound-shaped insects—looking not unlike pockmarks—on either the underside of leaves or the stems. Frequently they can be scratched off with a toothpick or removed with your fingernail. Or you could paint on and around the scales with a cotton swab dipped in methylated spirit. If that doesn't help, spray the plant with a garden spray containing dormant oils or a borax and kerosene combination.

Spider Mites are present when you see a fine web spreading across yellow leaves. You will see the mites if you shake a branch from the affected plant over a white piece of paper. They usually look like a red powder, like paprika, but sometimes they are brown or yellow. You can see the mites with a magnifying glass. In order to quickly rid your plant of this pest, you can use Metasystox-R (oxydemeton-methyl) or Pentac (dienochlor), an acaricide.

If you detect spider mites early, or if you want to follow up after treatment with a preventative, the use of predatory mites, the natural enemies of spider mites, is recommended.

Springtails live in, or on top of, the soil. They move about in a jumpy fashion. The presence of an individual insect is considered rather beneficial; however, when they appear in large numbers, they become pests, because then they attack the roots. Springtails only multiply in wet soil. To get rid of them, treat the plant with a household spray.

Whiteflies are often found on *Sageretia*, pomegranate, and hibiscus. They thrive best in stale air and a dry environment. Their larvae and eggs usually hide on the underside of leaves. The tops of the leaves sometimes show a yellow sprinkling. You can combat this pest with its natural enemy: the ichneumon wasp. In addition, a garden spray with an oil emulsion or a contact insecticide is very helpful, as are organic preparations of pyrethrum and the yellow sticker cards.

Mealy bugs look like little cotton balls sitting on the axil of branches, twigs, and leaves. The small insect hides in the center of the cotton ball and is protected from predators by a waxlike covering. Treat the infested plant with a pyrethrum spray or other contact insecticides. Mealy bugs have no natural enemy.

Root mealy bugs can cause yellowing leaves and often kill plants. If you take the tree out of its container and examine the roots and find whitish-grey clumps that look like cotton balls, your plant is infested with this insect. You can use diazinon to combat root mealy bugs. When the infestation is severe, water the soil with a solution of Metasystox.

In general, when combating pests that have invaded your bonsai plant, keep in mind that, wherever there is soil, there is life, and not everything that moves is dangerous. Over time you will develop a keen eye and learn to detect what is dangerous and what is not. Some species react badly to some pesticides; check with a nursery before you use one, if possible.

Whenever you make a decision to use a particular preparation, don't stop treatment too soon—even when you think you have won the battle. Continue treatment two or three more times. Then you can be sure that the eggs that some pests might have left behind are also killed.

Be sure to keep all pesticides and other chemicals out of the reach of children and pets, in clearly marked containers. Read and follow the instructions carefully, and remove people and pets from the area when you apply the chemicals. Spray in a well-ventilated area. Protect yourself with gloves and a face mask.

Planting and Repotting

Young as well as mature bonsai plants must be regularly transplanted. This is very important for the development of small trees for the following reasons:

High time to transplant.

- The soil is used up after two to three years, in quality as well as quantity. The plant has used up everything that it can. The pH value of the soil has changed; the ability of the soil to let air and water through has diminished; the amount of soil has decreased. The plant has literally eaten the soil. Furthermore, the roots have filled the whole container.

- The roots need to be cut back. It is necessary to cut back the root system of every mature bonsai plant every two to three years by one-third. It encourages new root growth and reestablishes the proper proportion between the crown and the root ball. In addition, make sure that all dead root fibres are removed.

- Some plants need a new larger container every now and then to give their roots more space. This is particularly important for young, fast-growing bonsai. The size of the new container depends on how much the tree has grown.

- Young bonsai that got their start in a flowerpot should be transferred to a bonsai bowl. When a shoot has grown to a certain stage in a normal plant pot, further growth can be slowed by transplanting to the more limited space in a bonsai dish.

Roots are cut back by about one-third.

The best time for repotting is the start of the active growing cycle, which is, of course, in the spring. There is an exception to this rule: when the plant is in bloom, transplant after the plant has finished blooming.

How often you should transplant depends on the species of plant. A young and fast-growing bonsai needs a root cut, a larger container, and new soil every year; repot older plants every 2 to 3 years; evergreens need repotting only every 5 years. However, when it comes to repotting, the bonsai gardener should rely more on observation and experience than on strict rules. When, for instance, the roots have grown to such an extent that the root ball begins to be pushed upward, it is high time to transplant.

Handling Plants When Repotting and Cutting Roots

Allow the soil to become somewhat dry before repotting; this makes it easier to remove the old soil. Before starting, in order to avoid exposing the roots to the air for too long, have all your tools and the new container ready.

First, lift the whole tree (roots and all) out of the container. Clean the old container carefully if you want to use it again, to avoid transferring any diseases or pests that might be in the old soil.

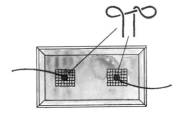

Plant your bonsai in its new container, covering the drainage holes with a plastic mesh; secure each plant with a wire loop so it won't move. You can use the ends of the wire to secure the plant in its new container. This is not necessary if the bonsai remains indoors rather than outdoors, where it is subject to winds and the weather.
Wenn Sie eine sehr flache Schale ausgewählt haben und befürchten,

If you plant your bonsai in a deep container, put a ⅞" (2 cm) layer of gravel on the bottom for good drainage; this will prevent the root ball from standing in wet soil.

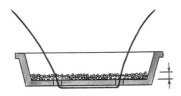

Then add a thin layer of soil on top of the gravel.

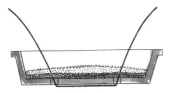

Take the whole plant in your hands, and, using a small piece of wood (like a chopstick), remove the old soil from within the root system. Then cut the roots back by ⅓ to ½.

Removing a bonsai from its pot and preparing the new container with mesh and wiring, gravel, and soil.

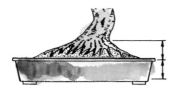

Place the bonsai on top of the soil in the container, but not exactly in the center. Make sure that the top of the root ball, just beneath the trunk, is positioned above the edge of the container. In order to improve new root growth, you can arrange the roots evenly around the trunk.

Difficult-to-arrange root branches can be secured with wire clamps.

Wires inserted through the drainage holes can be used to secure the plant.

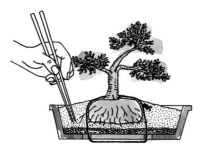

Now start filling the container with new soil, using a wooden stick to move the soil into the spaces between the roots. Push the soil around the plant with your fingers, up to ¼ inch (½ cm) below the edge of the container.

Smooth the surface of the soil, arranging the soil a little bit higher around the base of the trunk.

Planting the bonsai in its new container.

Now the bonsai must be watered generously so that the wet soil is washed into the spaces that remained between the roots. For the next couple of days, water sparingly, because the roots are not yet able to absorb much water or nutrition at this point. Do not fertilize the repotted plant for at least six weeks.

The Proper Soil

Never reuse old soil when repotting a bonsai. It doesn't have the necessary nutrients; isn't "clean," meaning free from bacteria; it won't let sufficient water run through; and it is too compacted to allow oxygen to penetrate. It is easy to mix bonsai soil if you know the proper combination. Bonsai soil usually contains a mixture of loam, sand, and humus. The loam (a natural mixture of sand and clay) acts like a buffer; sand loosens the soil and makes it possible for water and oxygen to penetrate (the drainage effect); humus, among other functions, is important as a culture medium for the bacteria necessary for life. Humus is, for instance, present in peat moss and in the soil on the forest floor.

The best mixture for your indoor bonsai consists of 3 parts crumbling loam, 5 parts peat moss, and 3 parts sand. For azalea and all other bonsai in need of a more acidic soil, the mixture is as follows: 1 part loam, 5 parts peat moss, and 2 parts sand. All the ingredients mentioned are readily available in nurseries. Crumbling loam can also be found in open fields. Of course, you can always buy ready-made bonsai soil. A favorite is a mixture of lowland and highland peat moss, vermiculite, washed sand, ground brick shards, powdered seaweed, and granulated loam. It is further enriched with nutritional and trace elements. The pH value of this mixture is suitable for almost all types of bonsai. However, it contains too little acid for azalea and must be supplemented with more peat moss.

Tools Needed for Repotting

When you get ready to transplant your bonsai—if not before—you will realize the importance of having the necessary basic tools on hand. Have these tools ready before you begin:

- A pair of all-purpose bonsai scissors for root pruning, which are also used to cut shoots, twigs, and thin branches

- A pair of pliers for cutting thick roots—those close to the root ball

- Plastic mesh for covering the drainage holes

- Anodized aluminum wire of various gauges.

• A root comb—or a chopstick—used to separate matted root fibres

• A bonsai broom, used to clean off and smooth out the surface of the soil.

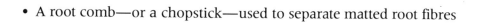

• You probably already have a watering can with a head that produces a gentle shower, as well as a spray bottle. If not, it would be a good idea to get both items now; they are necessary for the proper daily care of your plants—not only after they have been repotted.

If you take good care of your tools, they will last for a long time. Cleaning the tools with an alcohol-moistened rag and oiling them whenever it becomes necessary are the best means to ensure their long life.

Shaping and Creating

Look at your trees. Each lives its own life; they don't know each other.

—A teacher of Zen Buddhism

Learning from the Masters—Step by Step

Giving form to something alive is never arbitrary. For this reason, we express our feelings for these small trees by trying to discover their essence with sensitivity and by trying to make this essence visible.

When creating indoor bonsai, we look for guidance to their big brothers outside in nature. However, it is not a matter of copying, but rather the art of getting to know the characteristics of each tree and bush in their clarity and simplicity, and letting this be our guide in giving each small indoor plant its individual shape.

If we look around a park or a mixed forest, we will notice the many different basic shapes of trees and bushes and the principles underlying their creation. In spite of the different "personality" of each tree, each species has its own typical characteristics: the way the branches are arranged, the distance between the ground and the

Top: A shade-providing tamarind tree, surrounded by rice fields.

Bottom: A mixed growth (deciduous and coniferous) forest in the fall.

Ficus virens growing over a rock.

first branch, the development of the trunk, and the shape of the crown. The more familiar you become with the basic forms of trees in nature, the better able you will be—when looking at your bonsai—to recognize its essential form.

A bonsai master places the bonsai tree at eye level and looks "inside." He will take time and allow himself peace and quiet when observing his plant. Let the masters inspire you, and be guided by their experience in cutting, tying, bending, and wiring.

Basic forms of trees, as can be observed in nature and already-shaped bonsai plants, was the inspiration for the sketches on pages 33 to 36.

Formal Upright. The branches grow symmetrically in every direction; the lower third of the trunk in the front has no branches.

Informal Upright. The trunk is curved, becomes narrower at the top. Branches grow outwards and to the back.

Coiled. The trunk, becoming narrower towards the top, twists around its own axis. Such trees can grow in many different directions.

Exposed Roots. Here, the exposed roots are seen below the lower portion of the trunk. The mangrove tree, with its stilt-like roots, was the model for this bonsai form.

Weeping Willow. A tree, growing more or less upright, which has downward trailing branches, like a willow.

Broom. From a straight, upright trunk, the branches all grow from the trunk to the same height. This form is reminiscent of a straw broom.

Globe or ball shape. *Densely growing branches on a straight, upright trunk create a ball-shaped crown.*

Umbrella. *Many tropical trees develop huge, shade-providing, umbrella-shaped crowns.*

Cone-Shaped. *This tree is slender and absolutely straight, like, for example, the cypress tree.*

Literati Style. *The trunk grows freely, either upright or leaning slightly to one side; branches grow only on the upper third of the trunk. This form allows for the utmost in artistic expression.*

Windswept. *Branches grow only in the direction in which the tree is leaning, as if it had been whipped into this shape by high winds.*

Slanted. *Similar to the windswept form; however, the branches grow in all directions. The roots are more developed on the side to which the tree is leaning, and are more exposed there.*

Half-Cascade. *The models for this shape in nature are trees that grow horizontally over the edge of cliffs. The top of the crown is just above the edge of the container or a little beyond.*

Cascade. *The models for this shape in nature are trees that grow over the edge of a cliff with their branches cascading downwards. The trunk and the branches of this bonsai grow down far below the edge of a usually deep container.*

Double or Twin. *Two trunks with different diameters and heights grow from a single root system; their branches alternate symmetrically and harmoniously.*

Multiple. *Several trunks grow from one root system, creating a small group of trees.*

Raft. *The trunk is laid horizontally in the container, from which the roots develop. Branches—looking like individual trees—grow upward.*

Forest. *Several species of trees—differing in age, height, and trunk thickness—are planted in one shallow container.*

Clinging to a Rock. Trees grow roots in small hollow spaces or cracks in a rock.

Root over Rock. The roots of the tree grow around a rock and down until they reach the soil in the container beneath.

Pruning

One of the most important parts of bonsai gardening is the pruning of branches, shoots, and leaves. The goal is not only to keep the plant small and to create balance or a form that is characteristic for the plant, but also to keep the plant healthy and growing. Here, you will see the individual steps.

Cutting Branches and Twigs

If you want to create a bonsai from a young plant, you must first perform what is called the basic cut. Here, too, we must consider an important tenet of bonsai culture: that understanding the character of the tree-to-be is more important than rigid adherence to a rule. Therefore, the suggestions that are offered are only intended as a guide.

Generally speaking, whenever you decide to prune a tree, you must make sure you have enough time. Look at the plant often while pruning. Look "into" the plant, imagining how the form will change if twigs and branches are removed.

In the beginning, it takes courage to prune. But you will find the necessary courage and confidence when you realize that capturing the essentials is what determines the character of these small trees.

The Basic Cut

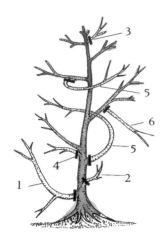

1. Remove all branches from the lower third of the front of the plant. The front side of a bonsai tree is the one that lets you look "inside"; it's the side where much of the shape of the trunk and branches is visible.

2. The branches of a bonsai should not point forward, but rather to the sides and the back. Only in the upper part of the crown are small branches and twigs permitted to grow forward.

3. Cut one of two branches located at the same height opposite each other, removing the one that doesn't conform to the right–left sequence.

4. Cut one of two branches that have grown directly on top of one another.

5. Remove the branches that grow to the other side past the trunk.

6. Remove the branches that grow downward.

Before (top) and (bottom) after pruning. The numbers in the top drawing refer to the steps in the list at right.

Pruning branches and twigs expertly is illustrated in the photos at the left.

- Small twigs are cut off close to the trunk with a pair of pruning scissors.

- Heavier branches are removed with concave bud-removing pliers. These pliers leave a small indentation behind, which heals well, leaving only a small scar.

- Very heavy branches are first sawed off, and the part remaining is best removed with concave pliers. It's a good idea to cover the larger cuts with tree wax.

Pruning Shoots

By cutting back and removing shoots, the bonsai gardener preserves as well as changes the shape of trees, fostering growth and health. Generally speaking, shoots are left on the plant only when they are to grow into a new branch—if the direction in which they will grow is correct. This is easy enough to determine since shoots are always cut above the stem of a leaf and where the stem is already pointing in the direction that the emerging branch will grow.

When pruning horizontally growing branches, make sure you observe the direction of growth. Before and after pruning: Left: Correct; Right: Incorrect.

Cut made above a stipule and bud.

New shoot that grew after pruning.

Always make your cut in the direction that the new shoot is growing. Generally, prune the top 1 to 3 leaves (or pairs of leaves) after at least 6–8 pairs of leaves have developed and the shoot has already become slightly lignified (woody). But do not cut too close to the stem of the last leaf or pair of leaves, in order to avoid damage to the bud at the axis of the leaf. It is possible, however, to cleanly remove a leaf bud.

Pinching a terminal bud.

Always remove those shoots that are of no use to the tree. "Of no use" means they are wilted or dead, they are too close to another shoot or branch, or they interfere with the view of the trunk.

Expert pruning of shoots keeps your bonsai looking young and beautiful because it encourages the formation of new buds as well as delicate branching of the crown.

Pruning tropical plants can be done almost any time of the year, since they grow actively all year round. In the case of subtropical bonsai, the best time for pruning them is during their main growing period, during spring and summer. The only exception is the time when your plant is in bloom; plants in bloom should not be pruned.

Before pruning.

After pruning.

Trimming the Leaves

Leaf trimming is very important for achieving a well-balanced small tree. The goal is to create more and smaller leaves, thereby achieving a balance between the size of the trunk, the branches, and the crown of the tree.

Since leaf trimming is a very stressful process for a small tree, bonsai gardeners recommend that it be done in two stages: the first cut is followed by the second after about 14 days. At the first cutting, remove only the largest leaves. However, if your plant is strong and healthy, you can remove all the leaves at one time.

Top: This Ficus religiosa has been stripped of all its leaves. Bottom: Six weeks later, the leaves have grown back; however, they are much smaller than they were.

Before the cutting.

New shoots that grew after the leaves were cut.

Always trim the leaves so that a small piece of the stem remains, because a new shoot will develop at this point, called the sprout axil. The proper time for cutting leaves is the spring.

When you have finished trimming the leaves, remember that the plant needs very little water, because some of the plant's digestive "organs" have been temporarily removed.

Sometimes an indoor bonsai doesn't look very attractive right after it has been stripped of its leaves, but you will be rewarded later, because the trunk, branches, and twigs will have much more pleasing proportions.

Schefflera arboricola, a beautiful indoor bonsai, belonging to David Fukumotu, Hawaii.

Plant with air roots.

Pruning Roots and Air Roots

Regular trimming of the roots has already been discussed in the previous chapter under "Repotting." At this point we add a reminder that there is a balance between the root system and the crown of the tree. Vigorous trimming of the roots always obliges you to trim the crown of the tree also.

One of the elements of the form of a tropical bonsai is its air roots. They are left undisturbed to develop freely, adding to the exotic appearance of the plant. If they grow vertically into the soil or alongside the trunk, they also transport nutrients to the plant. Air roots that seem to interfere visually or appear too dominant in relation to the overall tree can be cut off without doing damage to the plant.

Increasing the Circumference of Trunks and Branches

Sometimes a trunk or a branch of a tree may seem too small in proportion to the rest of the branches and twigs. Increase their circumference and make them stronger! The basic principle is very simple: Branches, twigs, and leaves draw the nourishment necessary for growth from the soil—not only for their own development, but also for the trunk of the tree. If the trunk is too thin in relation to the crown, leave in place the branches that are closer to the ground—those that you would normally remove when pruning. They provide nutrition for the lower part of the trunk, thus increasing its size. Once the trunk has reached the desired size, those low branches may be cut off.

Proceed in the same manner with branches and smaller twigs. If you let the branches, shoots, and leaves grow naturally for a while, they will grow stronger.

Here, the lower right branch is left on the tree until it has reached the proper thickness and better proportions with the rest of the tree. Only then is it pruned.

Binding and Bending

A Chinese bonsai gardener shaping a boxwood (Buxus) with strings and cotton bandages.

As the art of bonsai developed over time, new methods of shaping and creating were added to the traditional techniques. Binding and bending are two such methods, and, when they are handled expertly, a gardener is able to achieve stunning results. The essential ingredients necessary for the job are patience, reflection, and knowing the load-bearing capacity of your small tree—in other words, true bonsai talent. The goal of bending and tying might be, for instance, to change the distance between branches.

Another way to influence the shape of a bonsai is to bend the branches and twigs downward, closer to the ground. The following examples may serve as a guide. When bending and tying, it is important to remember to cushion the places where the string or wire touches the branch. A piece of rubber or cloth will serve as a cushion.

Here, branches of an elm are pulled downwards with bonsai wires fastened to the container.

To increase the distance between two branches, you can wedge them apart with a small piece of wood:

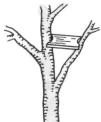

To bring two branches closer together, you can bind them together with string.

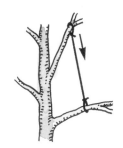

To bend down a branch, you can tie a weight to it, for example, a stone:

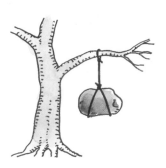

To have several branches bending down further, tie them to the trunk or to the edges of the container with string:

Wiring and Shaping

You can change the direction in which a branch, twig, or shoot wants to grow by wrapping it with wire and bending it into the direction of your choice. The wire should remain in place until the branch or shoot is growing in the direction that you have chosen— a process of cautious adjustment that is, however, only possible if a special technique is applied.

Experienced bonsai gardeners make use of this method when they, for instance, want to bend a branch downward that is very straight and rigid, so that the tree will look older than it really is, or when they want to straighten out crooked branches or twigs. Gardeners will put up with the fact that their wired indoor bonsai will lose some of its beauty for anywhere from ½ to 1½ years; that's how long

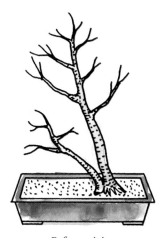

A Ficus benjamina 'Natascha, shaped with wires.

Before wiring.

After wiring.

wiring might take, almost as long as children have orthodontic braces on their teeth.

The effects of even minimal wiring and shaping are often much greater than an inexperienced bonsai gardener might expect. This is because, when only a few branches are wired, you allow more light to reach the inside of the tree, which in turn allows those branches and twigs within the grown to develop better, which changes the form of the tree.

Wiring, therefore, is not a technique that interferes with the development and growth of a tree. On the contrary. The only exception is when branches are bent down. This *will* slow down growth and development. Make sure, therefore, that the shoots at the end of a branch that is forced down are always pointing slightly

The author in the process of wiring a small tree.

With a wire-cutting pliers, the wire is cut close to the trunk without damaging the bark.

upward. This is a sure sign that the branch is not drying out or dying off.

It's important that you use the proper wire of the proper thickness. The best wire is anodized aluminum wire. This wire is easy to bend and is not noticeable, because of its dark color.

The wire you use should be about one-third the thickness of the branch or twig that is to be wired. The wire should also be about one-third longer than the branch or twig. A small assortment of wires of varying gauges should be part of the tools and equipment of the bonsai gardener.

Small corrections using the wiring technique—a good way for a beginner to practise the method—can be done throughout the year. Shoots, however, should only be wired after they have ripened, meaning after they have begun to lignify. More extensive corrections should be done between fall and spring, or before the main growing phase. The wires should not be tied too tightly around the branch or twig, and bonsai gardeners recommend covering the wire with thin paper before wrapping in order to prevent damage to the tree. Observe the plant closely so that you will be able to react right away to small damages in the bark. Should you detect any damage, loosen the wire, even if the desired shape has not yet been achieved. Wiring two or three times in succession won't harm your indoor bonsai. You will harm your tree if you have to tear out a wire that has become embedded in the bark, however.

If, in spite of every precaution, a wire has become embedded after all, remove the portion that is *not* embedded with a wire cutter and leave the rest in the bark. There are many venerable, beautiful, old indoor bonsai that have been living well even with a piece of wire embedded in the bark.

It is also important to take a gentle approach when shaping a branch or twig wrapped in wire. It's helpful to test how far a branch or twig will bend "without pain" before wrapping the wire around it. Should the branch split anyhow, cover the injury immediately with tree wax, and, in the case of a larger injury, wrap it with raffia.

The following examples will show you the most important wiring and shaping techniques:

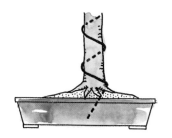

Wiring the Trunk.   The end of the wire is pushed at an angle into the soil at the back of the tree. Use a thick wire for wiring a trunk.

Wiring a Branch.   Even if you want to bend only one individual branch, the opposite branch must also be wired—it secures the wire. Start to wire in the middle of the branch whose direction you want to change. The angle of the wrapped wire should be 45°, and the distance between the turns should be even.

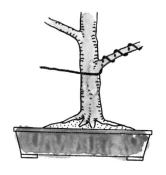

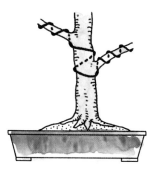

The trunk, branches, and twigs are always wrapped in the direction of their growth: from below upwards. Don't leave the end of a wire loose; cut if off at the back of the branch or twig.

Wiring a Twig.   The thinner the twig, the closer you need to wrap it. Extremely thin twigs—those that are still green—should not be wrapped.

Make sure that you don't trap leaves under the wire.

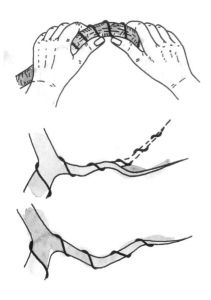

When bending a wired branch use the necessary force to accomplish the task, but be gentle. Use your thumb as a counter pressure to the force applied with your hand. This will prevent breaking or splitting.

Don't try to force a branch against a bend it has grown into naturally. Always keep the original direction of growth in mind when bending a branch.

The first bend of a branch should be made close to the trunk, and the first bend of a twig close to where it grows out of a branch. Whenever a branch is bent downwards, it should, at the same time, be bent forward.

Tools for Forming and Shaping

The basic tools a bonsai gardener needs have already been discussed in the previous chapter in the section on repotting. What follows is a list of tools necessary for pruning, bending, wiring, and shaping.

- A narrow, long-handled pair of bonsai scissors for cutting shoots and thinning the crown of a tree

- A wide-handled pair of scissors—a practical tool with many different uses

- A pair of root-cutting pliers to remove thick roots growing close to the root ball

- A bonsai saw for removing thick branches

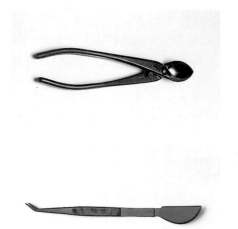

- A pair of concave cutting pliers for cutting branches close to the trunk—to allow for faster healing

- A pair of bonsai tweezers to remove young shoots, wilted leaves, and, possibly, to pick off pests and insects

- A pair of bonsai cutters to cut off leaves and shoots

- Different gauges of anodized aluminum wire: 1–6 mm.

- A pair of wire cutters to cut wires close to a branch or twig without damaging the bark

As you accumulate more and more tools over time, don't forget to take good care of them. Occasionally sharpen the cutting edges of your tools. Regular cleaning with an oil-dampened cloth takes no time at all.

Antique bonsai bowl, approximately 120 years old, from the pottery city of Fushan, China.

A view inside the Bonsai Museum in Heidelberg.

The Bonsai Container as a Design Element

The art of creating unique, beautiful ceramic containers for bonsai plants by hand has been a long-standing tradition in China and Japan and is as old as the art of bonsai itself. In the West, many countries by now have famous collections of precious bonsai trays and bowls; some are very simple, while others are richly decorated.

The container for a bonsai plant is often compared to the frame for a picture. As with the frame of a work of art, the bonsai container can complement the character of a plant or serve as a counterpoint to the whole. Choosing the right container, in terms of size, color, and shape, for a specific bonsai tree is a highly developed art.

To develop an eye for the proper container, look at photos in bonsai books and walk through bonsai exhibitions or a bonsai museum. But, as with cultivating a bonsai, no rigid rules exist when it comes to choosing a container. It is only important that the plant and the container together create a harmonious whole.

Handmade pottery bowls by Peter Krebs, Herborn, Germany.

We basically distinguish among round, oval, rectangular, square, six- and eight-sided containers, and containers that are shaped like a flower. They may be deep or shallow, have a flat bottom or have feet, and be glazed and decorated or plain.

The more sure you are about what kind of container you want, for the plant as well as for the ambiance of the room where the plant will be, the more patience is required to find the right one. Strolling through a good specialty store will surely be worth your while. The gardening store of a botanical garden is another likely place to look for containers.

Regarding container selection, we have a few basic suggestions that might be helpful for the beginner; bonsai gardeners can expand the list as they accumulate more experience. Here are a few examples:

Ficus religiosa

- For a formal, upright form, a flat oval or rectangular container is best.

Vitex quinata.

- A twin-trunk tree with a heavy crown needs a heavy container as a counterbalance.

Ficus nanda.

- This cascading plant shows up well when potted in a deep container.

Gardenia jasminoides.

- Indoor bonsai in bloom and plants with light green leaves profit from a glazed container in a light color.

Casuarina equisetifolia.

- A dark-leafed or coniferous indoor bonsai is set off to best advantage in a brown, red, or grey container.

As a rule, the length of the container should be two-thirds of the height of the bonsai tree. If the indoor bonsai is wider than it is tall, which is seldom the case, choose a container that is two-thirds as wide as the plant.

The depth of the container should be proportionate to the diameter of the trunk, or, in the case of a group of trees, the diameter of the trunk of the largest tree. The sides of a container may be straight, on an angle, rounded, or flowing. A container with straight sides is best for a bonsai that has a strong "personality," while round containers complement softer and slanted forms. With flat, rectangular, and oval containers, the longer side is always considered the front side.

By the way, when choosing a container always make sure that the inside of the container is not glazed.

A painted antique container from Yixing, China, 18th century.

An antique container from Yixing, decorated with Chinese writing.

A 120-year-old container whose colors and embellishments are typical of the pottery town of Fushan, China.

An old porcelain bonsai container from China.

Two 150-year-old bonsai containers from Fushan, China.

Flat containers that are either square or six-sided usually are placed with straight side facing the front. However, the container can also be turned so that a corner is facing the front.

If a container is very deep, either a straight side or a corner can face forward. Deep six- and eight-sided containers are positioned so that a corner is facing the room.

It is not unusual for true bonsai enthusiasts, who have made their indoor bonsai part of the ambiance of their home, to develop another hobby: that of collecting old, valuable containers. Old, handmade pieces, with their classical beauty, by far outshine even precious modern bowls. Old containers may be decorated with ornaments, elaborately shaped, made of porcelain, or be painted. However, the most impressive seem to be those that, following in a rich tradition, have been created in stunning simplicity.

Practice Makes Perfect

If I knew that the end of the world would be here tomorrow, I would go outside and plant my little apple tree today.

—Martin Luther

Creating Four Classic Bonsai Forms

The form a bonsai tree can take on depends less on the species of the tree than it does on the tree's individual personality and the preference of the bonsai gardener. This age-old adage of bonsai-culture wisdom is vividly demonstrated in the examples that follow. Here we see different ways of shaping a *Ficus benjamina* 'Natascha' and a *Hibiscus*. Four times the bonsai gardener was inspired by the natural characteristics of the plant.

Hibiscus schizopetalus, informal upright form.

Ficus benjamina, ball-shaped form.

Ficus benjamina, twin-trunk.

Ficus benjamina, multiple trunk.

Informal Upright Form

The informal upright is one of the most elegant and favorite bonsai forms. Its bends are typically larger and more pronounced at the lower part of the trunk and shorter at the upper part. The outside of the trunk supports branches while the inside does not. To achieve the informal upright form, the bonsai gardener can use two methods. The trunk may be wired and shaped or, without wire, using the binding method, shaped into the desired form. On the following pages, you will be shown the second method. Select a *Ficus benjamina* 'Natascha,' or any other plant. The trunk should still be flexible and should already have a slight curve. Bending the trunk will increase this already existing curve.

Li Vei Xing is about to shape his favorite plant, the hibiscus, into an informal, upright form.

Begin by inserting a stick in the soil about ¾ inch (2 cm) away from the trunk. The trunk and the stick are loosely tied together at the lower fourth of the tree. Holding the trunk at the midpoint of the tree, push it down with gentle force. The trunk will bend to one side. This is the first curve, which is tied to the stick at the point where you were holding it. Secure it well, because the string has to hold a curve that the tree is not used to yet. Next, repeat the process in the upper part of the plant, where the trunk is thinner and more flexible; bend and tie the curve to the stick. You should have created a smaller curve that continues the S-shaped lower curve.

Right: The tree, before tying, already has a slight curve. Far right: the tree, tied to a stick for the first curve, is bent again to form the second curve.

Remember, when tying the trunk or branches to a stick, that the plant will stretch out somewhat when the tie is later removed. Therefore, you should tie a deeper curve than you eventually want to achieve.

Next, remove branches, twigs, and leaves:

- from the bottom up to the first curve

- at the inside of the curves

- all branches and leaves that are in the immediate vicinity of the trunk

- all large dark-green leaves, and, as the last step, shorten new growth so that the tree develops a dense crown.

Depending on how extreme the curves of the trunk are, the branches remaining on the plant will have a tendency to grow upward to some extent. However, they can be wired and gently bent horizontally or downwards.

Left: The tied tree before pruning. Middle: unnecessary twigs, leaves, and branches have been removed. Right: the tree, transplanted into a bonsai container, will eventually retain its curves after the stick has been removed.

The plant should remain tied and, if necessary, wired for about 6 months. Normal care and regular pruning continues as usual. After 6 months, you can remove all ties and wires and then plant your bonsai in a carefully chosen container.

Ball-Shaped Form

With experience, bonsai gardeners can visualize the shape that they want a plant to grow into, even before they start. This is particularly the case with the ball-shaped form. The goal is to create a clean form: a straight trunk free of branches with a dense, ball-shaped crown. This is possible if the gardener keeps to the "golden section" ratio when shaping and pruning: ⅓ trunk and ⅔ crown.

First, remove all branches and twigs from the lower third of the trunk. Next, trim back new growth and thin out the crown, which means removing twigs and branches that cross each other or are too close together. Such pruning encourages growth and assures that the crown grows into the desired shape. Cut off any large, dark-green leaves.

Left: the unpruned tree. Middle: the lower ⅓ of the branches have been removed. Right: the tree, planted in a bonsai container, has leafed out.

Now plant your small tree in a bonsai container and care for it as you would any other indoor bonsai. Remember to remove new shoots regularly.

Twin-Trunk Form

The art of bonsai begins with the choice of the plant. Here, we have a good example. For a double- or twin-trunk bonsai, we need a plant that has two trunks from one base: one taller and thicker and, if possible, not growing parallel to each other.

If need be you can take *two* plants and place them in the desired relationship to each other in one container:

- The first step is—as already mentioned—to remove all branches and twigs from the lower ⅓ of each trunk. The result is that—automatically—the small trees will have branches only above the lower ⅓ of the trunk, a very important detail in the overall shaping.

- Next, remove all branches and twigs on both trees that seem to grow into each other.

- In order to achieve the classical two-trunk form—in other words, to emphasize the effect of both trunks—remove those branches of the larger tree that grow directly above the smaller tree. This opens up the crown, allowing a view through the leaves.

Left: a twin-trunk plant. Right: the twin-trunk plant sometime later, in its bonsai container.

The next step is to prune the branches and the twigs, keeping in mind the goal, which is the creation of a pyramid shape for both trees. This means that the lower branches are the longest; the branches become shorter and shorter as they reach the top of the plant. Instead of a pyramid, you may, of course, also create other forms for the crown, such as a ball or an umbrella shape. What is important is that the two trunks appear and remain separate and that the overall shape of the crown gives the impression of coming from one tree. As we have already mentioned, branches and large leaves growing close to the trunk should be removed. The plant is then transplanted and cared for in the usual manner.

The Multiple Trunk Form

If you have a plant with several different-sized trunks growing from one root system, looking like a bouquet of flowers, you have the makings of a multiple-trunk plant. These types of plants are frequently available at nurseries. However, make sure that the trunks

Left: a multiple-trunk plant before pruning. Middle: after pruning. Right: the plant in its bonsai container, sometime later.

do not cross one another and that the distance between them is unequal.

- Start by removing all branches and twigs on the lower third of all the tree trunks.

- Remove most of the leaves, leaving only those that are small and light green. This will give you a view inside the crown and a sense of the crown's natural shape.

- Remove all branches and leaves that interfere with the shape you desire: that of a bouquet of flowers.

- Trunks that are straight or growing in the wrong direction are wired and bent into the desired form. With the *Ficus* and related plants, you can influence their direction of growth without wiring. By repeatedly and patiently bending their branches, you will get the configuration you want. Now transplant the plant you have shaped into a decorative container, where it will grow and develop.

Miniature Landscapes

The rock, the green, overwhelming feelings . . . in your spell, words disappear.

—Liu Dschang-King

The Art of Creating Masterful Indoor Bonsai Groupings

During the Tang Dynasty, when the fine arts in general were at a peak, the bonsai culture also developed to new heights. For the first time, whole landscapes were planted on a tray.

The planting and cultivation of miniature landscapes combined with great imagination the observations that gardeners made of nature and architecture. The creation of Chinese bonsai landscapes, almost playful in design, does not and never has adhered to formal rules, often including small, artistically created clay figurines, houses, temples, and water.

From the Chinese miniature landscape, the classical, austere group and rock plantings were a natural next step, which developed later in Japan. Many variations on this theme are possible; however, they must include only three elements: plants, stones, and earth.

A beautiful forest created with several pomegranate trees.

A Small Forest In the House

For every bonsai enthusiast, particularly for the "old hand," there comes a time when creating an indoor forest is a must. Such creation brings into the house the exotic charm of a rain forest or the dream of having a romantic grouping of several trees.

Particularly suited for an indoor forest are small-leafed plants, such as the small-leafed *Ficus*, *Serissa*, *Carmona*, myrtle, or elm.

Plants as young as two to six years old can easily be used to create an indoor forest, which means that you don't have to spend a fortune. The minimum number of trees is 5, better yet, 7, or 9, or more, of different heights and trunk size. Most important, it must be an uneven number.

A very important tip: if you want to create a mixed forest, choose plants that have the same or similar needs. If they are not compatible on that score, it will become very difficult to care for your forest.

When you plan your forest and start looking for bonsai trees, keep in mind how groups of trees appear in nature. In nature, every tree is different. For instance, one tree might be the "father"—that is, distinctly larger and stronger than the others—tempting you to arrange the grouping like a family photo. But it is best to disregard this idea, which suggests that the smallest ones are always in front.

In the case of an indoor forest, it is just the opposite, because the smaller ones are planted behind the tall ones, which gives a group of trees more depth visually. Even more interesting effects can be created if you use ferns and other low-growing plants; they provide variety to the landscape and replicate the floor of the forest as it is found in nature.

Imagine that you are looking over the shoulders of a bonsai master planting an indoor forest, as you carry out each step in planting your own. For this small forest, choose nine *Ficus neriifolia* plants (rubber trees) of differing sizes and heights. Plan your forest as you would the building of a house. Choose a container with care, one that is rather plain or, in any case, flat.

You will need some low-growing plants as well as soil. Have all the necessary tools at hand: container, earth, mesh, wire, a pair of root cutting pliers, a pair of bonsai scissors, and wooden picks. Reread the part of the book on repotting (pp. 26–30), but don't feel restricted by too many rules. Your indoor forest is going to be a huge success!

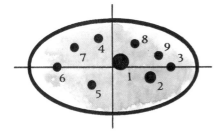

Diagram of plant dish and tree placement, from tallest tree (1) to smallest (9).

Draw the outline of the container you are going to use on a piece of kraft paper, or newspaper; then copy the arrangement of the trees (including the numbers), shown in the drawing at the left, onto your drawing.

Prepare the container by placing the mesh over the drainage holes and filling the container with bonsai soil, about ⅜ inch (1 cm) deep.

Prepare the plants by taking them out of their pots, cutting roots back by a third, and removing large leaves and branches that you don't need or that are too long.

Line the plants up according to their height.

Now you can begin to plant the first tree. On the sketch you have drawn on the paper, it is #1.

The trees that are planted on the outside are turned so that their strong branches are pointing to the outside. Use more soil as needed.

When all the plants are in place, water thoroughly; you may also fertilize at this time. All you have to do now is care for your little forest as you do any other bonsai: water carefully, less rather than more, and keep it in a bright location but not in direct sunlight. New growth (new leaves and roots) is a sign that the plants are doing well. At this point, you may increase watering and feeding, as recommended. Your forest needs to be transplanted after two years—just like the other bonsai plants. The trees will have developed one root system and should be treated as one plant. Pruning the roots is done as usual.

Indoor forest from one Casuarina equisetifolia

From One Indoor Plant, A Forest Grows

Nature possesses boundless imagination when it comes to growing things, and most of the time we only become aware of it when we take up gardening as a hobby—when we try to imitate it. Creating a bonsai forest—growing a group of trees in one container that originate from an individual potted plant—rests on two principles: (1) thin branches and twigs will develop roots when put into the soil (the principle of layering); and (2) branches always grow upwards, towards the light.

The *Ficus benjamina* 'Natascha' is, for example, a houseplant well suited for creating an indoor forest. This is the way to proceed:

Look at the plant and determine which is its "good side," meaning the side with the longest and most numerous branches, since these are the branches that later will grow upwards.

Cut off all small twigs and leaves that grow in the immediate vicinity of the trunk. Wire the whole trunk from the base to the tip so that you can bend it.

Branches and twigs that can easily be bent towards the "good side" (see the bottom photo on this page) are tied together loosely with bonsai wire. The more branches you can tie together, the more trees you will have for your little forest. The top of the tree is bent to the left.

Remove the branches that remain on the "thin" side. Make sure that the lower third of the branches that you have tied together are free of small twigs and leaves. With a sharp knife—on the bare side of the trunk—remove about ¾ inch (2 cm) of bark every 1¼ to 2 inches (3 to 5 cm) (top photo). The trunk will develop roots from these incisions when they come in contact with soil.

The plant prepared in this way is now removed from its container. Reduce the root ball drastically, leaving only enough root fibres as are necessary for the tree to be supplied with a minimum amount of nutrition.

The trunk and the remaining root ball are now planted horizontally in a long bonsai bowl or a flower box and covered with about 1¼ to 1½ inches (3 to 4 cm) of soil.

The finished forest after two months in a bonsai container.

Build a little mound around the root ball. The branches and twigs remain tied together until they are used to the new direction in which they are to grow and are able to support themselves. In about 4 to 6 months, this little forest will most likely be able to maintain itself through newly formed roots. When transplanting, check to see if they are there. If so, you may cut off the old root ball. Once your indoor forest is transplanted into its new container, its care is the same as for all your other bonsai: in the beginning, water sparingly, and for 6 to 8 weeks do not expose it to direct sunlight. Regular pruning of the individual trees will make your bonsai forest more beautiful and denser.

Top: Ficus neriifolia forest.
Bottom: Cupressus pyramidalis forest.

Carmona, ferns, and clover planted on rocks.

Bougainvillea, cultivated over a rock.

Rock Planting

There are two basic forms:

1. Plants that grow *on* a rock—with their roots growing in the soil embedded in the rock's crevices. The bonsai arrangement is situated in a low, shallow container filled with water or sand.

2. Plants that grow *over* the surface of a rock. The plant sits securely on the rock, and the roots, while clinging to the rock, grow down into the soil, from which the plant gets its nutrition. A plant with long, strong roots must be chosen for such a planting; for instance, all types of *Ficus*, *Schefflera*, *Carmona*, and *Serissa* are well suited.

Clinging to a Rock

Plants that grow out of a rock do so literally without ever coming in contact with the ground. Look for stones with a rough surface that also have crevices, ridges, and cracks. Any well-shaped stone will do. You can find them in nature, but they can also be bought at a bonsai specialty store. If the crevices in the rock are not deep enough for holding the necessary roots and earth, do not hesitate to use a hammer and a chisel to make them bigger. The shape of the rock determines how the plants are arranged. Start by first placing three wire loops in each indentation or ridge where you intend to put a plant (two-component epoxy resin stone glue is good to attach them).

The loops should form a triangle large enough to accommodate the root ball of the plant. Now cover the cavity with a ¾-inch (2 cm) layer of peat moss–loam mixture (50:50), place the plant with the root ball into the cavity, and secure it with the wire. Do not cut the roots that extend beyond the cavity, but rather spread them over the rock and cover them with the peat moss–loam mixture.

After the bonsai plants are in place, do the secondary planting as follows: plant low-growing, but fast-growing creeping evergreen plants, which will prevent the loss of soil when you water. The best plants used for this outdoors are mosses; however, they do not grow too well indoors. Here, *Soleirola*,  *Pilea microphylla*, low-growing ferns like *Selaginella*, or coral moss like *Nertera* are much better. These plants are also secured to the rock with wire loops.

The secondary planting should include only low-growing plants. Cut them back, as you would your lawn, whenever they get too tall.

Place the planted rock on a tray filled with either water or sand. Flood the rock often, since rocks have a tendency to dry out quickly. Water carefully to prevent loss of soil. Feed your bonsai-rock landscape for the first time after about 8 weeks with liquid fertilizer. It is necessary to replace lost earth from time to time.

The longer you live with your landscape, the more you look at it, the more interesting it will become; sometimes you might see it as an island, a mountain, or even a rocky coastline.

Root Over Rock

One day you may find a particularly beautiful rock and—more often than not— that will be the beginning of an interesting, perhaps whimsical, bonsai landscape. Look closely at your find, and determine which side should face the room. Remove the plant you have chosen from its container,

wash its roots, and determine its most beautiful side. This will be the side of the plant that faces the room. Place the plant on top of the rock, and pull its roots over it and down so the ends extend beyond the rock. Now wrap the rock with a soft material, but tightly enough to hold the roots in place. (A plastic bag cut into strips makes good wrapping material.) Make sure the roots on the rock are completely covered.

The reason for wrapping the rock is that the wrapped roots are kept in place. It also prevents the roots from developing new little roots on the rock instead of in the soil.

Now "plant" the rock with its exposed roots sticking out below in a bonsai container or a flowerpot filled with bonsai soil. The height of the container should be the same as the height of the rock. Cover the roots extending beyond the rock with soil, press down firmly, and water generously. In about one-half year, depending on

the type of plant, a root ball may have developed under the rock. Carefully remove the rock with the plant from its container, remove the plastic bandage and those roots that are small and dried out, and carefully, gently clean the roots on the rock.

Transfer the rock and plant—after careful pruning of the root system—to an appropriate bonsai container. Add a secondary planting. After 6 to 8 weeks—when the low-growing plants have established new roots—you can start regular care.

Sometimes a bonsai gardener wants to grow a particular plant over a particular rock even if the roots are not long enough to reach the soil and won't be able to get the necessary nutrition. You can overcome this problem by placing the rock with the plant in a heavy plastic bag with a few drainage holes (see far left). Fill the bag with equal parts of peat moss and sand or ready-made bonsai soil.

Left: bonsai and rock in a plastic bag. Right: the turned-down bag exposes more and more root and rock.

About every 8 to 12 weeks, turn down the plastic bag by 2 inches (5 cm) or so, removing the excess soil around the roots on top. In this way, the plant and the rock "grows" slowly out of the bag. An increasingly larger portion of the roots become exposed, and the roots that are still covered grow faster. The small tree is ready for transplanting when the plastic bag is only 2 inches (5 cm) tall and most of the roots are exposed.

Picturesque Indoor Bonsai for a Healthier Indoor Environment

The basic idea is very simple: the climate in our houses, particularly during the heating season, is frequently dry and unhealthy. Most of the humidifiers are technical monsters that use a lot of energy, are aesthetically not very appealing, and their value, as far as our health is concerned, is very controversial. Containers filled with water have none of the negatives but are in general not very attractive. Enthusiasts of indoor gardening have a simple plant "humidifier," which not only improves the environment but adds charm to the indoor bonsai you already have.

The Small Water Garden

Those of us who don't like appliances and are creative can plant both easy-to-grow and more demanding plants in a simple container filled with water and let that be our alternative to an electric humidifier. Such a container, when placed between or near other bonsai plants, conveys a sense of quiet as well as drawing

Pilea microphylla, growing on a rock in a water-filled tray.

A small water garden, with a stone and various aquatic plants.

attention to the small trees that are close to it. Water gardens can round out the natural appearance of an indoor collection, giving it an added charm and serenity.

A water garden can include many different plants and beautiful rocks, providing a perfect arena in which to be playful and imaginative. The number of plants that grow well and are comfortable in this natural humidifier is large: water grasses, water lilies, and many more (see the list below). If these aquatic plants become too tall, just cut them back. The necessary nutrition is provided exclusively through the water; for this reason, the water level should never be too low. A water filter can be used to soften the water and provide nutrients.

Aquatic Plants

Latin Name	Common Name
Acorus gramineus var. pusillus	Grassy-leaved sweet flag
Althernanthera sessilis	—
Eleocharis acicularis	Hair grass, Slender spike rush
Gymnocoronis spilanthoides	Red parrot leaf
Hydrocotyle verticillata cv. 'Cardamine'	Water pennywort
Ludwigia glandulosa	False loosestrife
Ludwigia mullertii	False loosestrife
Lysimachia nummularia	Moneywort, Creeping Jennie
Lysimachia nummularia aurea	Moneywort, Creeping Jennie (yellow variety)
Marsilea drummondii	Water clover, Pepperwort
Micranthemum umbrosum	—
Myriophyllum brasiliensis	Water milfoil

The Water Fountain Garden

The water fountain garden is an interesting and very beautiful way to improve the climate in your home. Even if it is a bit more complicated than the water garden, it's worth it. The fountain consists of a rock on which plants grow and from and over which water flows.

- Look for a well-shaped rock, and choose a container whose base is at least twice as big as that of the rock and about 2 inches (5 cm) deep.

- Drill a hole in the rock. This hole must be large enough to accommodate a small electrical pump.

- From the indentation that holds the pump to where the water is to exit, drill a connecting channel wide enough to accommodate a water hose, usually ⅝ to ¾ inch (1.5 to 2 cm) in diameter.

- To take full advantage of the water-fountain technique, first: make sure that the electrical pump is energy-efficient, UL approved, and maintenance-free. Now, insert the water hose, with a filter, in the channel you drilled from the underside of the rock.

- Next, place the rock asymmetrically, as with all bonsai plantings, in the water-filled bowl, and attach your plants as described earlier under "Rock Planting." Fill small indentations in the rock with low-growing plants, which are particularly beautiful as they "play" in the water. Plants listed in the Aquatic Plants Table are well suited for secondary plantings. They can be planted so that they grow in the water, with some attaching themselves to the rock, increasing the charm of your creation.

The water filter is situated in a place where it cannot be seen. It softens the water and provides nutrients. Most water filters must be replaced twice a year.

When everything is in place, the water is pumped over the edge of the rock, creating a charming, playful scene, while adding humidity to the air.

If you replenish the water as needed and replace the nutrition-supplying water filter, the water fountain will serve you well, and your plants will stay healthy. One more tip: make sure that you clean the water filter regularly.

From the Beginning...

...and suddenly I felt the desire to be a tree.

—*Maeda Yugure*

Propagating Your Own Indoor Bonsai

To see a plant come into being and see it grow is one of the most rewarding experiences you can have. Most gardeners who have experienced the nurturing and creation of bonsai will, at some point, want to start from the beginning. All that is needed is patience, regardless of which of the many possible methods you choose.

Indoor Bonsai from Seed

Imagine looking "into" one of your charming bonsai plants and being able to remember the many different stages of development you have witnessed ever since the first green shoot appeared above the soil. For the amateur gardener, this is the ultimate reward.

Raising a bonsai from the very beginning—which takes many, many years—has been passed on to Westerners by Japanese bonsai gardeners, who call this process *misho*.

Ficus benjamina, grown from seed; about 15 years old.

Many varieties of seeds are available. Of course, they can be collected from the tropical fruit and nuts that we buy throughout the year, such as lemons, avocados, pomegranates, and pistachios. Seeds are also available in specialty stores.

Don't be confused when you read on a package "bonsai seeds"; it simply implies that the plants raised from them are particularly well suited for bonsai. Many of our favorite houseplants can be raised from seeds and transformed into bonsai plants.

The fresher the seeds, the more easily they will germinate. Some seeds must be soaked before planting. Put them into a jar of water (those with hard shells are nicked) and leave them in the water for

Fruit Whose Seeds Can Be Grown as Indoor Bonsai

Name of the Fruit or Nut	Plant's Latin Name
Carambola	*Averrhoa carambola*
Cherimoya, Chirimoya	*Annona cherimola*
Lemon	*Citrus limon*
Lime	*Citrus aurantiifolia*
Sweet orange	*Citrus sinensis*
Durian	*Durio zibethinus*
Soursop, Guanabana	*Annona muricata*
Pomegranate	*Punica granatum*
Common guava	*Psidium guajava*
Carob, St. John's bread	*Ceratonia siliqua*
Pitanga, Surinam cherry	*Eugenia uniflora*
Loquat, Japanese plum	*Eriobotrya japonica*
Litchi, Leechee	*Litchi chinensis*
Golden-shower	*Cassia fistula*
Indian laburnum	
Pistachio	*Pistacia*
Rambutan	*Nephelium lappaceum*
Sapodilla, Nispero	*Achras zapota*
Tree tomato	*Cyphomandra betacea*
Tomato tree	

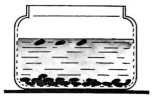

24 hours. Seeds that are ready for planting have soaked up water and will be at the bottom of the jar; those that are floating on the surface are dead. Sow the seeds while they are still wet; they can't be allowed to dry out after they have been removed from the water bath. Sow the seeds in a glass container about 3¼ to 4 inches (8 to 10 cm). You can also use a bonsai bowl. Whichever container you use, make sure that it has drainage holes on the bottom. Of course, the holes need to be covered with a plastic mesh to keep the soil from washing out. Individual seeds can be sown in a flowerpot.

Seeds germinate best in nutritionally poor soil, to which no fertilizer—or at least very little—is added. The sprout is surrounded by fertile tissue and feeds itself. A mixture of relatively fine-grained peat moss and sand, or soil prepared specifically for transplanting, is suitable. Of course, you can also mix your own: one part sand and one part peat moss. What is most important is that the medium be free of disease-causing bacteria. This means that you should never use previously used soil.

To plant seeds, fill the container you have chosen with the growing medium, up to 1¼ inches (3 cm) below the rim. Place the seeds on top, and cover them with an even layer of the medium. Larger seeds should be pushed into the soil slightly. Smaller seeds should be covered with the medium the following way: put the medium in a strainer and shake it over the surface in a thin layer. The layer of soil covering the seeds should not be thicker than the thickness of the seeds themselves.

If you want to prevent new, emerging shoots from falling over (a fungus disease called "damping off"), sprinkle them with a solution of chinosol. Keep the soil in the container evenly moist and out of direct sunlight. The proper temperature for germination ranges from about 64 to 72°F (18 to 22°C). Spraying or submerging the container in water is the best method for keeping the soil moist. Watering the conventional way often results in the seeds being washed out of the soil. Submerge the container up to ¾ of its height in a bowl of water (the water should be at room temperature). The soil absorbs the water through the drainage holes. Covering the container with a piece of plastic will prevent the soil from drying out too fast. Keeping the temperature around the seeds—and, later, the sprouts—constant decreases the time needed for germination.

As soon as sprouts have developed 4 to 5 leaves, they can be transplanted. It is recommended that young shoots be fed, at the earliest, after a month. Use only half the amount of fertilizer recommended on the container, and organic fertilizer is best.

Once young plants have reached about 3¼ to 4½ inches (8 to 12 cm), you can begin to influence their development. Removing the very top shoot encourages branching. Begin to shape the plant in bonsai fashion after the plant is about 6 to 8 inches (15 to 20 cm) high and its branches have begun to lignify slightly. Of course, you will choose the most beautiful, sturdy plant.

Three- and four-month-old tamarind seedlings.

Indoor Bonsai from Cuttings

You probably already know what a cutting is: a shoot or branch removed from the mother plant and either placed in a glass of water or planted directly into the soil for rooting. Cuttings may be taken from a tropical or subtropical plant, or a potted indoor plant. Creating a bonsai plant from a cutting doesn't require quite as much patience as starting it from seed. The best time for taking a cutting is during a plant's active growing period. However, you can cut a shoot

any time during the year, as long as it is at least 2 to 6 inches (5 to 15 cm) long or has at least 4 to 6 leaves or pairs of leaves. In addition, the shoot should already have begun to lignify slightly at the base; in other words, it should not be soft. It is important that the shoot or branch be cut off properly. With a sharp knife or a pair of bonsai scissors, cut directly below the leaf bud, and remove leaves on the lower ⅞ to 1¼ inches (2 to 3 cm) of the stem. The latter will prevent the stem from rotting in the soil. Shorten the tip of the shoot if it is still soft.

Cuttings taken from some houseplants—for instance, from a *Sageretia*—should be immersed in water until they have rooted sufficiently. With a clear glass container, you have the advantage of being able to observe the development of the roots. However, don't use a container with a narrow neck; you might damage the roots when you take the cutting out. A waterglass is best. Place the glass on a windowsill where temperatures are between 64 and 75°F (18 and 24°C).

Cuttings from many tropical and subtropical plants may be planted in the soil immediately after having been cut. The emphasis is on "immediately," because the cut surface must not dry out. The exceptions are cuttings from succulents, like jade plants. With them, the cut surface has to dry out—for about 14 days—before they are planted in dry soil, and they should not be watered until the first tiny roots have developed.

Here is another insider tip: in order to encourage root development, you can dip the cut surface of a shoot, branch, or twig in a growth-hormone powder.

Left: Packing soil lightly before transplanting seedlings.
Right: Keeping seedlings under a cover to ensure enough moisture.

You can transplant your cuttings into flowerpots, bonsai bowls, seed dishes, or wooden flower boxes. Just be sure they have drainage holes, which must be covered with a mesh. Fill the container to just below the rim with a peat moss–sand mixture. Pack the soil down slightly with a wooden board, and insert the cuttings ⅜ to ¾ inch (1 to 2 cm) deep. Make sure there is enough space between each plant; their leaves should just barely touch each other. After planting them, thoroughly water them and, to prevent the water from evaporating too fast protect them with a clear plastic bag or a clear glass cover. Put this "miniature greenhouse" in a place with sufficient light but not in direct sunlight. Temperatures between 64 and 75°F (18 and 24°C) are ideal. New leaves are a sign that the cuttings have grown roots. The plastic or glass cover can then be removed. After 2 to 3 months, you can check carefully to see whether the cuttings have developed a root ball or not. If they have, the plants can be transplanted into small flowerpots.

Three-month-old rooted cuttings, planted in plastic pots.

Indoor Bonsai Through Air Layering

Air layering is another method used to create, in a relatively short time, "old" bonsai plants. With this technique, you can create a separate new plant from a branch of a particularly beautiful houseplant that looks like a potential bonsai candidate. This can be done any time of the year, but spring is recommended. The thinner the branch you have chosen, the faster the process.

Air layering can be done on many species. Three ways of beginning are:

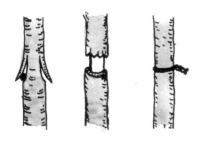

- Make ¾ inch (2 cm) cuts on either side of a branch, opposite each other as shown in the drawing at the left. The cut surfaces are treated with hormone rooting powder and the bark is kept away from the branch by inserting a little pebble or a piece of peat moss between them.

- Remove a band of bark about ⅜ to ¾ inch (1 to 2 cm) wide.

- Wrap a piece of wire immediately above the place where roots are to develop. The pressure of the wire cutting into the bark encourages root development.

Let's describe one method in detail. Remove about a ¾-inch (2 cm) strip of bark at precisely the place where the roots are to grow. Wrap

Four stages in air layering: (1) cutting the bark; (2) wrapping the cut area; (3) the rooted cutting; (4) the new bonsai in its container.

the bare spot with peat or sphagnum moss as follows: wrap the place where the bark was removed with a piece of plastic bag below the cut; fill this "bandage" with the damp medium, and pull the plastic over it; and tie the top of the plastic securely to the stem. Clear plastic allows you to watch for root development. Until roots have developed, the peat or sphagnum moss has to be kept uniformly moist. If necessary, water the plastic "cuff" from the top.

While the new small tree is still attached to the mother plant, you can already start pruning and shaping it. Depending on the species of plant, in about 6 to 12 weeks, roots should have grown sufficiently to enable the new plant to live on its own. Remove the "cutting" from the branch just below the newly developed root ball, and transplant it either into a flowerpot or directly into its bonsai container. Allow the peat or sphagnum moss to remain around the roots. Treat your new bonsai plant like any other transplanted bonsai.

Collecting Plants

For centuries, bonsai gardeners have collected plants from the outdoors whose growth already has been stunted due to climate and other environmental influences. The plants then are transplanted into containers for their gardens. Gardeners preferred those plants that naturally had small leaves and fruit and a compact root system. Even after many years, we often are able to detect the wild past of those precious and revered bonsai. Wind and weather have shaped them in a way that could never be artificially duplicated. However, we can also collect young plants and make them into bonsai, not only those that have gone through the experience naturally. Bonsai enthusiasts are still able to find subtropical plants in the wild that are well suited for a transformation to an indoor bonsai, for instance, on vacation in subtropical regions. (Many countries, including the U.S., forbid bringing soil or tree and shrub seeds in from another country, as they may transmit diseases. Be sure to find out if it is legal to bring plants home if you travel from one country to another.)

Experienced bonsai gardeners travel with a somewhat strange assortment of "tools" when going on a plant hunt: a collapsible spade, a pair of bonsai scissors, and a small crowbar, for digging in rocky terrain. In addition, they will have a watering can and a spray bottle to keep the plants they have dug up moist. They will also bring plastic bags and newspapers (an alternative to peat moss).

Three steps in digging up a potential bonsai. Width of the circle dug should correspond to the widest part of the crown.

The best times to collect outdoor plants are during the spring and fall. But with very special care, plants collected during a summer vacation have been known to develop into beautiful indoor bonsai. Of course, if you are on vacation, collecting should be done on the last day of your vacation in order to shorten the stressful time for the plant. If you have discovered a suitable plant, remove about ⅓ of its leaves as well as all unnecessary branches; this will reduce transpiration. It is very important that enough of the plant's root system, including the original soil, remain intact. It's particularly important not to harm the fine, fibrous roots that are necessary for transporting water and nutrition. To determine the proper size of the root ball, draw a circle around the plant that corresponds to the circumference of the widest portion of the crown or its branches. Cut into the dirt vertically with the spade—the deeper, the better. Carefully lift the root ball out of the earth, trying to keep it as undisturbed as possible. Place the plant on a plastic bag that has already been cut open and covered with the already damp peat moss or wet newspaper. Wrap and tie the root ball in the plastic. When transporting the plant, which is best done in a backpack, try not to shake the plant; protect it from wind and strong sunlight; and spray its leaves every now and then. When you arrive at home, immediately transplant the plant into a flowerpot, filling the empty spaces with the original soil that has fallen off the root ball with peat moss. Protect the plant for a couple of weeks from direct sunlight, and spray its leaves frequently. It will take about 6 to 12 weeks until the plant is used to its new home; wait until then before fertilizing. This is also the time when the plant is ready for the first step of bonsai pruning: it is transplanted into a bonsai container, which, of course, also includes root pruning.

Conscientious bonsai gardeners and nature lovers will never indiscriminately rip plants from the wild. Rather, they will carefully make sure that the gap created by digging up a plant is closed by new growth, and that the plant they intend to take home has a better-than-average chance of surviving. Also, be certain that the plant you want to remove is not under protection, and that it may be taken out of its environment. Be sure to get permission from the person on whose land your prospective bonsai is growing before you begin, also.

Of course, many bonsai enthusiasts would prefer to shape and create their small trees without too much preparation. If this is true for you, buy young bonsai plants that have been selected by bonsai gardeners, where the first stages of shaping have already been accomplished. Such plants, which are usually one or two years old, are already branching out and the "bonsai shaping" can begin. Start by shortening all new shoots. This encourages continued branching and creates a dense crown. After the plant is nice and bushy, you can begin shaping.

A 150-year-old elm tree that was found 40 years ago in the mountains of Taiwan and transplanted into a bonsai container.

Miniature Bonsai

The tallest are not the wisest . . .

—*Chinese saying*

The Smallest of the Small Are Becoming Popular

Like so many things in the high art of bonsai, miniature indoor bonsai also originated in Japan. If you have not held a real forest in the palm of your hand, you won't be able to imagine the charm of these tiny creations.

These tiny plants—varied in shape, planted in a variety of different containers, often planted as a decorative collection in a tray—are much more than just decoration.

Miniature bonsai are about 3¼ to 6 inches (8 to 15 cm) tall (some are even smaller), have the shape of a full-grown tree, and may live

A miniature Carmona and a miniature Sageretia, placed on a tray filled with sand.

A mini-azalea in an interesting handmade bowl.

in containers that are as small as an egg-cup. Several years and much patience is required in order to create these trees. Shaping and caring for them is no different from any other bonsai plant. Seedlings that are 1¼ to 2 inches tall (3 to 5 cm), cuttings with roots, or tiny plants found outdoors in nature can be the beginning. An experienced gardener can already see in such a tiny plant its potential for developing an interesting shape. The smaller the leaves, the more harmonious the proportions of the future miniature bonsai will be.

It takes about 3 years, sometimes 4 to 5 years, until a cutting becomes a miniature bonsai. However, the first signs of the shape of the future plant can already be detected after about 2 years. In shaping the bonsai, you should follow what you think is the natural shape of the plant. This should guide you from the very first pruning. From the very beginning—in order to keep the plant small—you must constantly remove large leaves as well as new shoots, except for one pair of leaves or one leaf. Slowly, the small plant will take on its individual form.

Today, bonsai shops carry mini-bonsai that have already undergone the first stages, and the gardener can take over from there, enjoying the step-by-step process of creating a fascinating plant in miniature form. The care of these plants requires a lot of devotion; because they have only a tablespoon of earth from which to draw nourishment, watering, fertilizing, and transplanting must be done much more often.

A miniature Sageretia in bloom, 3¼ inches (8 cm) tall.

The best way to water a miniature bonsai is to immerse the whole container in water— at least once a day. In order to keep the soil from drying out, mini-bonsai are often placed on a tray filled with damp sand.

This Ficus neriifolia was submerged in water until all air bubbled up from the soil.

Great care must always be taken when feeding, which is done once a week. It is best to use only half the recommended concentration of fertilizer and to add the fertilizer to the water bath used to water the plant. The soil should be slightly moist before fertilizing the plant. If you have an extremely small container, it's best to fertilize the plant from below, through the drainage hole, or with an injection needle. Of course, in this case too, the soil must be moist.

Because mini-bonsai containers hold so little soil, it is necessary to transplant often—approximately once a year. The roots should be shortened by ⅓ during transplanting, and feeding should be suspended for about 4 to 6 weeks; the nutrition contained in the new soil will last that long.

The Most Beautiful Indoor Bonsai from Around the World

Key to the Symbols

 Needs full, unrestricted light

 Needs plentiful water

 Needs a warm location during winter

 Thrives even with little sunlight

 Needs little water

 Should be kept cool during winter

Bougainvillea glabra
Paper flower
Family: Nyctaginaceae
Tropics

Bougainvillea glabra
Paper flower

The *Bougainvillea* originated in tropical Brazil and is by nature a climbing plant whose shoots can grow up to 13 inches (4 m) long. Today these plants are available in many different shapes and colors, and as houseplants.

Bougainvillea glabra has shiny green, slightly hairy leaves. Flowers appear in mid spring or early summer. The flower itself is inconspicuous, which makes the three surrounding colorful bracts, which look like three connecting triangles, that much more noticeable. In China, the plant is called "thorny azalea," since some of the older shoots grow into thorns. A *Bougainvillea* is relatively easy to transform into a bonsai, because its young branches and twigs are easy to bend and the plant is very robust. This bonsai plant should be placed outside during the summer so it will bloom.

Location: During the summer, the plant must be in a warm, sunny location outside; during the winter, it needs temperatures of about 49 to 54°F (6 to 12°C) and a bright, airy location. The winter is the plant's dormant period, when it loses almost all of its leaves. This rest period is necessary for the plant to develop its flower buds.

Watering: Very little watering is necessary during the winter; however, the soil should not be allowed to become completely dry. Increase its watering schedule at the beginning of spring. When the tree is outside and begins to form buds, the plant needs plenty of water. If you have a warm summer, immerse the pot in a water bath daily, until all air bubbles are expelled from the soil.

Fertilizing: From spring through summer, feed the plant once a week with liquid bonsai fertilizer—particularly when in bloom. Never fertilize during the winter rest period. Start feeding again in the spring, only when the first blossoms appear.

Transplanting: Every two years, and do root pruning at that time, either in early fall or before active growth sets in.

Soil: Use either bonsai soil or loam, peat moss, and sand at a ratio of 2:2:1.

Pruning: After blooming has stopped, prune vigorously, cutting back into the old woody part of the branches (late summer). Wait until 6 to 8 leaves appear, and then continue pinching back new growth regularly until the middle of spring, always leaving only 2 to 3 leaves in place.

Wiring: The easiest branches to wire are those that have begun to lignify. However, extremely woody or thick branches are almost impossible to reshape.

Propagation: This is best done with cuttings in a peat moss–sand mixture in spring or summer, or by air layering with peat or sphagnum moss.

Buxus harlandii
Boxwood
Family: Buxaceae
Subtropics

Buxus harlandii
Boxwood

The boxwood tree, usually the *Buxus sempervirens*, was known as far back as ancient Rome, where it was used for hedges. During the Baroque period and the Renaissance, boxwood were cut regularly to maintain the geometric shapes that were the fashion of the day.

The plant produces yellowish green flowers with an aromatic scent in early spring. Its fruit are oval- or round-shaped pods. Its leaves and roots contain the active substance "buxin," which was used in the Middle Ages for toothaches and as a treatment for worms. The boxwood grows to 3 to 10 feet tall (1 to 3 m) and does so very slowly. This plant does not like acid soil, does poorly in wet soil, and grows in full sunlight as well as in partial shade.

As of now, there are about 40 different varieties available in nurseries; most are *Buxus sempervirens*. The *Buxus harlandii* works best as a bonsai, because of its small leaves and attractive bark; it is also very tolerant of somewhat warmer indoor temperatures. In Taiwan, there are some wonderful and very old boxwood bonsai that were either created from garden plants or collected from the wild.

Location: During the winter, a cool spot is best—about 37 to 50°F (3 to 10°C). If no such spot is available, temperatures between 64 and 86°F (18 and 30°C) are also tolerated. However, the plant cannot be placed on or near a heat source. You must provide lots of fresh air! Place the plant outside after the last frost in spring; for the summer, in a sunny or partly shaded area.

Watering: Water moderately during the winter; during the summer, allow the soil to become somewhat dry before watering. Remove water from the saucer to avoid giving the plant "wet feet."

Fertilizing: Do not feed during the dormant period in the winter. Start again in the spring, and continue throughout the summer. Every three weeks, use liquid bonsai fertilizer, and once, during the active growing season, also use pulverized organic fertilizer.

Transplanting: Repot every 2 years, including root pruning, in late winter or in fall after the plant's growth period.

Soil: Use either bonsai soil or loam, peat moss, and sand at a ratio of 2:1:2.

Pruning: The branches can be cut throughout the year. Cut back new shoots to two to three pairs of leaves, after six pairs of leaves have developed.

Wiring: Wiring is possible throughout the year. After the basic shape has been established, individual branches and their leaves can be formed into cushion shapes by frequent pruning.

Propagation: Put well-ripened cuttings in a peat moss–sand mixture in late summer.

Calliandra haematocephala
Red powderpuff
Family: Leguminosae
Tropics to subtropics

Calliandra haematocephala
Red powderpuff

Tropical and subtropical regions in the Americas are the native habitats of the more than 120 different species of the *Calliandra* plant. But they can also be found in Asia and India. The *Calliandra* is a small, evergreen bush, with wonderful green, scented, double-feathered leaves that close up at night and when the plant experiences drought. The *Calliandra* grow pink to red powderpufflike flowers. The flower buds, which develop from late spring through summer, look like raspberries and grow from the leaf axils. From the flowers, the leathery leguminous fruit grows, bursting open when ripe and curling up afterward. The trunk of the young plant is light grey, turning dark grey to almost black with age. When transformed into a bonsai, this plant will brighten your home, adding a sense of the exotic.

Location: Indoors throughout the year is possible, but choose a spot that is light and airy. Put the plant outside by mid spring after danger of frost is over, in a partially shaded location. Do not place the plant on or near a heat source, but rather choose a spot that is light and somewhat cool—approximately 59 to 64°F (15 to 18°C).

Watering: Keep the soil evenly moist. Water less during the winter months if the plant is in a cool location.

Fertilizing: Use liquid bonsai fertilizer every two weeks during the growing season, from spring through summer; discontinue during the winter months. Adding phosphorus to the fertilizer increases blooming.

Transplanting: Transplant every two years, including root pruning, in the spring. Good drainage is important.

Soil: Use either bonsai soil or a mixture of loam, peat moss, and sand in a ratio of 1:1:1.

Wiring: Because the older branches break easily, wrap only young branches that are just beginning to lignify (summer).

Pruning: It is best to prune during the main growing season in mid spring and summer. Cut back new shoots to 1 to 2 leaves as soon as a shoot has developed 5 to 6 new leaves.

Propagation: This is best accomplished with seeds, or with cuttings from mid spring on in a sand–peat moss mixture of 1:1.

Camellia japonica
Common camellia
Family: Theaceae
   Subtropics

Camellia japonica
Common camellia

The *Camellia* originated in the mountains of Japan and Korea and grows there to about 33 to 39 feet (10 to 12 m). Today it can be found in Mediterranean countries, growing in gardens as trees or bushes, but only to 10 to 26 feet (3 to 8 m). It can be recognized by its shiny, dark green leaves and pinkish red blossoms. The *Camellia sinensis*, with its single and much smaller white flowers and yellow stamens, comes from Taiwan and India. It works much better as a bonsai than the *Camellia japonica*, particularly because its small white flowers and leaves are much better suited to the proportions of a bonsai plant. Most *Camellia* flower from late fall through early spring. They come in shades of pure white, pink-and-white speckled, golden yellow, and red, either single or double blossoms. This plant would be a wonderful addition to any bonsai gardener's collection.

Location: All tea plants (Theaceae) like an airy, cool location, with much light but not direct sunlight. Take the plant outdoors to a partly shaded spot in mid spring after danger of frost is over, and back indoors in early fall to a winter garden with an approximate temperature between 50 and 59°F (10 to 15°C); but the cooler, the better. Do not move the plant once the flower buds begin to appear, otherwise they might fall off.

Watering: Keep the soil uniformly moist. Increase watering during the warm summer months and while the plant is in bloom. If the plant is in a cold location, reduce watering. Use soft (decalcified) water.

Fertilizing: Feed every two weeks during the main growing period (after flowering has stopped) with liquid bonsai fertilizer. Do not fertilize during the winter months or when the plant is in bloom.

Transplanting: Repot every two to four years, depending on the age of the plant, in late winter or early spring, after its flowering period. This should be accompanied by moderate root pruning.

Soil: Use either bonsai soil or a mixture of loam, peat moss, and sand in a ratio of 1:2:1.

Pruning: In order to encourage branching, the new shoots of younger plants are pruned back, after they have developed at least four to six leaves, leaving only two or three leaves in place. When an older tree already has achieved the desired form and is about to bloom, prune only once, when the first shoots appear. Then leave new shoots in place so that the bush has enough time to develop its buds.

Wiring: The best time for wiring is during the fall and winter. If the plant has already begun to form flower buds, wait until it has finished blooming. Wire young twigs only after they have become lignified.

Propagation: Use cuttings that have become somewhat lignified, from winter to summer; root development is slow. Propagation by seed is also possible.

Carmona microphylla
Fukien tea
Family: Boraginaceae
Tropics

Carmona microphylla
Fukien tea

This is a tropical, evergreen shrub from southern China (Fukien Province). Its white flowers, which bloom almost the entire year, turn into light red berries. Its small, shiny, dark green leaves have little white dots on the surface, which are often mistaken for insect infestation. The trunk has a brownish red bark, presenting a wonderful contrast to its dark leaves. This plant works particularly well as a mini-bonsai. It is also a good houseplant, since it appreciates warm temperatures during the winter months.

Location: Keep the plant indoors all year, with temperatures around 50 to 75°F (10 to 24°C). It does well in a bright window but not in direct sunlight during midday (between noon and 3 P.M.) Find a partially shaded spot for it outdoors from late spring through summer.

Watering: Always keep the plant uniformly moist, because it will shrivel easily and simply stop growing if the root ball has been allowed to dry out.

Fertilizing: From early spring through summer, every 14 days with liquid bonsai fertilizer. During the winter, if the plant is in a warm location, feed it every six weeks. Water well before feeding to avoid root burn.

Transplanting: Every two years in spring, with moderate root pruning.

Soil: Use either bonsai soil or loam, peat moss, and sand in a ratio of 2:2:1.

Pruning: Regularly cut back new shoots to 2 to 3 leaves after they have at least 6 to 8 leaves. Branch pruning can be done throughout the year.

Wiring: In general, the *Carmona* can be easily shaped without wiring if you start when it is still young. But if you want to establish the basic form faster, the wiring method can also be used. Wiring can be done throughout the year; for new shoots, however, do not wire before the stems have become lignified.

Propagation: By cuttings throughout the year, although the best time is between mid spring and early summer.

Casuarina equisetifolia
Horsetail tree
Family: Casuarinaceae
Humid tropics

Casuarina equisetifolia
Horsetail tree

The horsetail tree originates along the sandy edges of the constantly humid tropics, from northern Australia to the Pacific islands to southeast Asia. It grows up to 82 feet tall (25 m) and reminds us, because of its slender shape, of a pine tree. Even so, it is considered deciduous, although its leaves look like pine needles. The name *Equisetifolia* means "horsetail leaves." Its flowers are very inconspicuous, and its fruit is a little cone that is about ⅝-inch (1.5 cm) in size. This plant allows the bonsai gardener to have a tree with needlelike leaves indoors; conifers, like pine, juniper, and others, don't do well indoors. This tree, however, is robust, and is most beautiful when cultivated as if it were a pine tree.

Location: The horsetail tree does well throughout the year indoors with bright light and lots of fresh air. During the summer months, it does best in full sunlight; during the winter months, temperatures between 50° and 60°F (10 and 16°C) with bright light are best. If the normal location is warmer, nighttime temperatures should be lowered to between 50 and 54°F (10 and 12°C).

Watering: In general, this plant should be kept uniformly moist. During periods of hot weather, it needs more water; however, do not overwater, because the roots have a tendency to rot. If the soil is too dry, the bark will shrink and the plant will die.

Fertilizing: Use liquid bonsai fertilizer every four weeks during the main growth period, from early spring to late summer. Do not fertilize during the winter months.

Transplanting: Repot every two years with moderate root pruning; make sure that the container is not too large.

Soil: Use either bonsai soil or a mixture of loam, peat moss, and sand in a ratio of 1:1:2.

Pruning: Cut back the branches in the spring when the shoots are well developed. The new shoots are always pruned when they are 3 to 4 inches long (8 to 10 cm), leaving them no more than ⅜ inch to ¾ inch long (1 to 2 cm). As soon as a cushion-shape growth has developed, new shoots can be pinched off by hand.

Wiring: It is best to wire in early fall, when the twigs have ripened.

Propagation: Use either seed or cuttings; the stems of the latter must be slightly lignified.

Crassula arborescens minor
Silver-dollar
Family: Crassulaceae
Subtropics

Crassula arborescens minor
Silver-dollar

The *Crassula* belongs to the succulents, which are at home in the semidesert and regions with similarly dry climates. *Crassula arborescens* are treelike, bushy, robust plants which grow to 6 to 10 feet tall (2 to 3 m) in their native habitat. The *Crassula arborescens minor* is a compact plant with small leaves, so it's a very good specimen for a bonsai. Because its treelike character is its natural form, good results can be achieved by just pruning it, making this plant perfect for the beginner.

Location: Indoors, this plant does well in a bright and sunny spot; outdoors, in mid spring—after the last frost—it does well in a sunny or partly shaded location. If the plant is exposed to direct sunlight, the leaves turn a reddish color and the plant remains more compact. Allow the plant to get used to direct sunlight slowly to avoid leaf burn. During the winter months, keep the plant indoors at temperatures between 46°F and 58°F. However, the plant can also tolerate temperatures from 61°F to 72°F (16° to 22°C).

Watering: This plant, like all succulents, needs little water. A good rule of thumb is to first allow the soil to become completely dry and then to water thoroughly. During the winter months, in a cool spot, water sparingly. Even during the summer months, the plant can be watered only every four to six weeks without suffering damage. (This is helpful when the gardener is on vacation!). Overwatering causes loss of leaves, and the roots begin to rot.

Fertilizing: From mid spring through summer, every 4 weeks, with liquid bonsai fertilizer. Do not fertilize during the winter months.

Transplanting: Anytime of year; approximately every 2 to 3 years, with minimal root pruning. Do not water for two weeks after transplanting.

Soil: Use either bonsai soil or loam, peat moss, and sand in a ratio of 1:2:2.

Pruning: It is preferable to remove the branches from early spring to summer. In order to bring out the natural character of this plant, remove all leaves at the lower part of the trunk and remove branches that are growing across one another and those that grow towards the inside. As soon as the new shoots have reached their appropriate size, pinch off their tips. After branching continues, shorten new growth, leaving only two to three leaves.

Wiring: Always appropriate, as soon as the branches or twigs have lignified. Be careful when wiring; the fleshy, soft branches are easily injured.

Propagation: This is best done with 2- to 6-inch-long (5 to 15 cm) cuttings from the top. Allow the cut surface to dry for 14 days. Then insert the cuttings in dry soil (peat moss and sand, in equal amounts). Water generously after the first white root fibres have developed, and keep uniformly moist.

*Cupressus macrocarpa 'Gold
Crest'
Monterey cypress
Family: Cupressaceae
Subtropics*

104

Cupressus macrocarpa 'Gold crest'
Monterey cypress

This cypress tree is a pyramid-shaped evergreen conifer; in nature, it grows up to 65 to 98 feet (20 to 30 m). It can be found in the Mediterranean countries as well as in Arizona, Mexico, and the Himalayan mountains. It flourishes in a warm, moderately light, dry place.

The Monterey cypress are much better suited to be bonsai than the green species are, since they tolerate heat better indoors during the winter months. Try to duplicate the natural pyramid form when creating this bonsai; the plant can also be easily formed into the formal upright shape, or used to make a small indoor forest. However, achieving the desired thickness of the trunk can be a problem. Since the trunk grows slowly when the plant is in a bonsai container, we recommend keeping it in a larger container for about 2 or 3 years until the trunk has reached the desired size.

Location: During the summer, keep this plant in a bright, sunny location indoors, or outdoors from mid spring (after the last frost), in a sunny, warm place. A partly shaded spot also is suitable. In the fall, or when the temperature drops below 41°F (5°C), place the plant in a bright location where the temperatures are between 41 and 59°F (5 and 15°C)—no higher than 68°F (20°C). Depending on the location, keep the plant moderately moist—somewhat on the dry side.

Watering: Water primarily during the main growing season in the summer. During the winter months, when temperatures are between 41°F and 59°F (5 and 15°C), keep the soil on the dry side, but never let it dry out completely.

Fertilizing: From spring through fall, feed once every 2 weeks with liquid fertilizer. During the winter, feed only when the plant is in a warm location and then only every 4 to 6 weeks.

Transplanting: Transplant every 2 years (including root pruning), in the spring.

Soil: Use either bonsai soil mixed with sand or a mixture of loam, peat moss, and sand in the ratio of 1:1:2.

Pruning: Pruning can be done throughout the year. The best time, however, is in the spring, before the main growing period. Always shorten new shoots by about a third.

Wiring: The best time for wiring is from the late winter to the early spring.

Propagation: Use cuttings that have partially ripened during the summer months; or use seeds.

Eugenia myrtifolia
(Syzygium paniculatum)
Australian brush cherry
Family: Myrtaceae
Subtropics

Eugenia myrtifolia
(Syzygium paniculatum)
Australian brush cherry

This beautiful evergreen tree, whose habitat is Australia, grows about 20 feet (6 m) tall there and has thin, elliptical, dark green, shiny leaves.

The flowers are white and similar to those of the myrtle, as they grow in clusters at the tip of short woody shoots in early summer. The fruit are small, egg-shaped, fiery red to lilac-colored, and are edible. If the leaves growing on the young shoots receive enough light, they become fiery red, and surely add to the charm of this subtropical plant.

Location: During the summer months, keep this plant indoors at a bright, sunny window, and be sure it gets lots of fresh air. Or else, take it outdoors from late spring through the summer; a sunny or partly shady location is suitable. During the winter months, it needs to stay indoors at a bright location, with temperatures between 59 and 64°F (15 and 18°C), although it will tolerate slightly warmer temperatures.

Watering: During the summer months, water generously, but always wait until the soil is somewhat dry before watering. During the winter months, of course, water less.

Fertilizing: From early spring through summer, feed every 14 days with liquid fertilizer; during the fall and winter, every 4 weeks.

Transplanting: Always transplant when the root ball has become very compact, usually every 1 to 2 years; include vigorous root pruning at these times.

Soil: Use either bonsai soil or loam, peat moss, and sand at a ratio of 1:1:1.

Pruning: Regularly cut back all branches and twigs that interfere with the desired shape of the crown to maintain a definite shape. New shoots that have 6 to 8 pairs of leaves should be shortened to 1 to 2 pairs of leaves.

Wiring: The branches and twigs that have become lignified can be wired; the best time is at the end of summer or just before the growing season in spring. Branches that you want to pull downwards can be wired and tied down throughout the year, however.

Propagation: With ripe cuttings throughout summer, or by seed in the fall.

Ficus buxifolia
Family: *Moraceae*
Tropics

Ficus buxifolia

The home of the *Ficus buxifolia* is Zaire—in other words, in the tropical belt of the globe. Its branches are slender, flexible, and relatively thin. Its well-shaped little leaves are leathery and dark green. This plant is very similar to the *Ficus triangularis*, but the leaves of *F. triangularis* are much longer. The *Ficus buxifolia* is especially well suited for creating bonsai, because it naturally has very small leaves and tolerates indoor conditions well. The *Ficus buxifolia* branches beautifully and, even as a young plant, produces small green fruit which grow in pairs from the leaf axils; however, in temperate regions, the fruits seldom ripen fully.

Location: This plant can be kept indoors year-round. During the winter months, keep it on a windowsill, which may be directly over a radiator, with temperatures between 64 and 75°F (18 and 24°C). The plant prefers a bright location, but it is also able to tolerate a somewhat darker spot. After the last frost in spring, a sunny or partially shaded location outdoors is ideal. When the temperature reaches about 59°F (15°C) in the fall, the plant must be taken indoors again.

Watering: As with all rubber trees, the soil needs to dry out before you water again. Too much water will result in the plant's losing its leaves.

Feeding: From spring through summer, every two weeks, with liquid bonsai fertilizer. During the winter months, every 6 weeks.

Transplanting: Transplant approximately every 2 years, and include root pruning if the root system is well developed; the best time is mid-spring.

Soil: Use either bonsai soil or loam, peat moss, and sand in a ratio of 1:1:1.

Pruning: Prune branches throughout the year if possible. New shoots, after having developed 10 to 12 leaves, should be cut back to the first 2 to 3 leaves. Since the trunk and branches are not very thick, we recommend allowing the main branches to grow until they have developed 30 to 40 leaves; if they are cut back then, the branches will have had a chance to become thicker. It is important to always remove branches that grow straight up also.

Wiring: Although wiring can be done at any time, the best time is during the active growth period. To create a formal upright tree, the trunk should be shaped when the plant is still young.

Propagation: This works best with cuttings during the summer, when temperatures are approximately 66 to 75°F (20 to 24°C).

Ficus carica
Fig tree
Family: Moraceae
Subtropics

Ficus carica
Fig tree

Fig trees have been cultivated for a very long time. They are related to the rubber tree, but with a difference: fig trees lose their leaves in the winter. The fruit (figs) were highly valued as far back as ancient times. Originally, their home was in the Middle East and the Mediterranean regions. The *Ficus carica* develops small fruit in the fall that become ripe the following summer. However, in some regions, few survive the winter. The leaves are deeply serrated and relatively large, but they can be significantly reduced in size if the plant remains in the same container for an extended period of time, providing the bonsai with better proportions. The plant also tolerates leaf pruning very well.

Location: Fig trees love full sunlight, particularly outdoors. Take the plant outside in mid spring and place it in the full sun. In early fall bring it indoors before the first frost, and keep it at temperatures between 41 and 46°F (5 and 8°C) or less, so that the plant can begin its dormant period. The less light the plant gets during the winter, the colder the temperatures should be. If the plant is kept indoors throughout the year, it needs a sunny, well-ventilated area at or near a window.

Watering: During the summer, the plant needs to be watered generously. But if you want to keep the leaves small, wait until they start to droop a bit before watering. If the tree is in a cool location during the winter, water sparingly but don't allow the soil to dry out.

Feeding: From the start of the growing period through summer, feed every 2 weeks with liquid fertilizer. The plant will be grateful if given an organic fertilizer in powdered form twice during the growing season.

Transplanting: Young plants should be transplanted every 2 years, older plants every 3 to 4 years. The best time is the spring, before new shoots appear. The fig tree tolerates vigorous root pruning well.

Soil: Bonsai soil to which a little sand has been added, or loam, peat moss, and sand at a ratio of 2:1:1.

Pruning: Fig trees can be vigorously cut back throughout the year. Prune back new shoots after they have developed 6 to 8 leaves, to 2 to 3 leaves. Throughout the summer, you may remove large leaves, which will encourage the growth of smaller leaves and improve branching.

Wiring: Although wiring can be done throughout the year, the best time is just before new shoots appear in the spring. It is very difficult to shape the branches of a fig tree, since they are very thick. Therefore, start early, while the plant is still young.

Propagation: In the spring, with cuttings; take them before they become lignified.

Ficus microcarpa
Family: Moraceae
    Subtropics

Ficus microcarpa

This evergreen tree, like almost all ficus trees, grows to immense height and has a huge, wide crown and many air roots. These roots grow from the branches down into the soil and take over the function of the trunk. This growth is similar to that of the legendary banyan tree (*Ficus bengalensis*), from whose air roots a whole forest of trunks may grow over time.

The *Ficus microcarpa* has been cultivated as a bonsai in southern China and Taiwan for many centuries. Its dark green leaves are similar to those of the laurel tree, and the color of the trunk is a beautiful whitish grey. The plant will tolerate somewhat low light and cooler temperatures. It is a robust tree that can be shaped into every conceivable bonsai form.

Location: It does well indoors throughout the year. During the winter months, it should be placed on or near a heat source (radiator) or on the windowsill, where temperatures are between 64 and 75°F (18 and 24°C). The brighter the location, the more vigorous the growth, and the more leaves the tree will produce. During the summer months, the plant can be moved to a sunny to partly shady location outside.

Watering: Generally, water only after the soil has become somewhat dry. The cooler the location, the less watering is required.

Feeding: Use liquid bonsai fertilizer every 2 weeks during the growing period, and every 4 to 5 weeks during the winter months.

Transplanting: Every 2 years, including root pruning. The best time is in the spring, but it can also be done in the summer after leaf pruning.

Soil: Use either bonsai soil or a mixture of loam, peat moss, and sand at a ratio of 1:2:2.

Pruning: The branches can be cut back any time during the year. New shoots are pruned to 1 to 3 leaves, after they have grown 6 to 8 leaves. At the end of spring, all leaves can be removed; this will improve branching. In any case, large leaves should be removed regularly to allow more air and light to reach the inside of the crown.

Wiring: Wiring can be done throughout the year, but not before the branches have become lignified. Remove wires early enough to prevent them from growing into the bark.

Propagation: This is best done with cuttings during the summer, when the temperature in the soil is around 75° (24°C), or with seeds. Air layering is also possible if enough plant material is available.

Ficus natalensis
Natal fig
Family: Moraceae
Subtropics

Ficus natalensis
Natal fig tree

This tree's habitat is South Africa (Natal). It is an evergreen and grows as a woody shrub or tree, with heavy branching, to heights anywhere from 10 to 65 feet (3 to 20 m). The leaves are shiny, dark green, leathery, and almost spatula-shaped, with a flat, slightly wavy tip. The fruit grow in pairs from the leaf axils. The bark is silver-grey with brown vertical stripes. If the humidity is high enough and if its branches are allowed to grow long enough, the plant will grow beautiful air roots that can be incorporated in the overall design of the tree. This tree needs little care, tolerates dry soil, and can be placed in full sunlight, but is also happy with less light. It can be vigorously pruned, and it can be shaped beautifully. When pruning is done properly, wiring is not necessary.

Location: Indoors at a window, with temperatures between 59 and 75°F (15 and 24°C). The plant can be near a heat source or on a windowsill without a problem. During the winter, the temperature should not fall below 54°F (12°C). During the summer months, after the last frost, the plant can be kept in a sunny to partly shady location outdoors. As soon as the temperature falls below 59°F (15°C) outside, the plant must be brought indoors.

Watering: Allow the soil to dry out somewhat before watering. During the winter, if the plant is in a cool location, water sparingly.

Feeding: Use liquid bonsai fertilizer every 14 days from spring through summer. Only feed the plant in the winter if it is in a location where the temperature is at least 64 to 75° (18 to 24°C).

Transplanting: Transplant every 2 years, in the spring, whenever the root ball is large enough and compact; include vigorous root pruning.

Soil: Use either bonsai soil or a mixture of loam, peat moss, and sand at a ratio of 1:1:1.

Pruning: This vigorously growing tree can be pruned throughout the year. When new shoots have developed 12 leaves, cut back, leaving only about 2 leaves on the stem. The best time for cutting leaves is in early summer.

Wiring: From mid to late summer, but only when branches and twigs are lignified.

Propagation: Propagate with cuttings in a peat moss–sand mixture in summer; the soil should be warm.

Ficus neriifolia
Family: Moraceae
Tropics

Ficus neriifolia

The *Ficus neriifolia* most likely developed from the *Ficus salicifolia*; however, the growth of the former is more compact and much slower. *Ficus neriifolia* have been transformed into bonsais in Florida for 30 years. Bonsai gardeners in Florida have produced very beautiful specimens.

This rubber tree has narrow, lanceolate, dark green leaves, similar in shape to the leaves of the oleander tree. The *Ficus neriifolia* develops a strong, straight trunk in a very short time. Its branches can be shaped into a beautiful umbrella-shaped crown, making the plant resemble its big brother, the shade-providing tree growing in the tropics.

Location: Indoors throughout the year. It loves having warm roots and a bright location. During the summer, it can be placed outdoors in a sunny or partly shaded area. When temperatures fall below 59°F (15°C) in the autumn, bring the plant back indoors and keep it at a temperature between 59 and 75°F (15 and 24°C). Moving the plant this way in the fall might cause it to lose all its leaves. However, at normal room temperature, they will grow back within 6 to 8 weeks. The plant also may lose its leaves if the location is too dark or too cold.

Watering: In general, water the plant only when the soil has become somewhat dry. If the tree has lost all its leaves, water sparingly until the leaves have grown back. Overwatering also causes leaves to drop off.

Feeding: Use liquid bonsai fertilizer every 3 weeks, except during the winter months, when it should be used every 6 weeks.

Transplanting: Every 2 years, including root pruning, in the spring; however, it is also possible throughout the year, except during the winter months.

Soil: Use either bonsai soil or loam, peat moss, and sand in a ratio of 1:1:1.

Pruning: The branches can be pruned throughout the year; shorten new shoots to ⅜ to ¾ inch (1 to 2 cm) after they have grown 3 to 4 inches (8 to 10 cm). All shoots growing within the crown, and those that grow straight upwards, need to be removed. Also, always remove large old leaves during the main growing period.

Wiring: Although wiring is possible throughout the year, the best time is during the summer. Repeatedly bending branches and thin stems by hand is also effective in shaping the tree into the desired form.

Propagation: With ripe cuttings in early summer, when temperatures are between 68 and 77°F (20 and 25°C). Air layering is another method that can be used, as long as the plant is tall enough.

Ficus religiosa
Bo-tree, Sacred fig
Family: Moraceae
Tropics

Ficus religiosa
Bo-tree

The *Ficus religiosa* is the holy tree of Buddhism. According to legend, about 500 B.C., Buddha had a revelation under this tree. That is one of the reasons why the bo-tree is often planted near Buddhist temples in southeast Asia. The leaves emerging on new shoots are reddish, providing the tree is kept in full sunlight. Old leaves have a very faint bluish tint. The leaves are heart-shaped with long tips. The trunk and branches have beautiful whitish grey bark. Older trees often develop a very decorative root system above the ground, which resembles intricate braids as it reaches the trunk.

The bo-tree works well as a bonsai. Beautiful specimens can be found in Thailand, but usually only in the gardens of real bonsai enthusiasts.

Location: This tree needs lots of light and warmth—in other words, the brightest location in your home, in full sunlight (at a window with a southern exposure). If possible, bring the tree outdoors by the end of spring, keeping it in full sunlight, but protected from wind. When temperatures fall below 60°F (16°C) in the autumn, bring the plant back indoors. If the temperatures are kept between 60 and 75°F (16 and 24°C), the plant can be placed near a heat source. If the location indoors is too cold and lacks sufficient light, the tree will lose its leaves.

Watering: As with all other *Ficus* trees, water only after the soil has become almost dry.

Feeding: Use liquid bonsai fertilizer every 2 weeks from spring through summer; during the winter months, every 6 weeks if the tree is in a warm location. If it is placed in a cooler spot and has lost all its leaves, feed only when growth begins again in the spring.

Transplanting: Every 2 years, in spring; include root pruning; make sure that the roots are evenly spread out on all sides. This will encourage the formation of a beautiful above-ground root system.

Soil: Use either bonsai soil or loam, peat moss, and sand at a ratio of 1:2:1.

Pruning: The branches may be pruned all year long; shorten new branches to 2 to 3 leaves as soon as 6 to 8 leaves have developed. If placed in the right location, this *Ficus* will grow vigorously, which makes it possible to strip all of its leaves twice during the growing season. The result is that the new leaves that grow back will be much smaller and the overall branching will be improved.

Wiring: Wiring can be done throughout the year, but only wire lignified branches. Remove wires early enough to prevent injury and scarring.

Propagation: With cuttings in early spring, when the soil temperature is between 71 and 79°F (22 and 26°C). Seeds are very difficult to buy.

Ficus benjamina
Benjamin tree
Family: Moraceae
Tropics

Ficus benjamina
Benjamin tree

Ficus benjamina, also called "weeping fig" because of the shape of its crown and roots, is one of the best-known rubber trees, of which there are more than 500 species. Originally native to India and Malaysia, the tree is found today in almost every tropical region, where it grows into a tall tree with a huge crown. The drooping branches give it an elegant appearance. The leaves are ovate, light to deep green, and slightly wavy. The tree produces small, figlike, green fruit that turn blood-red when ripe. In many regions, the *Ficus benjamina* has been used as a houseplant for a long time. Its robustness and tropical appearance account for its popularity. Although many varieties exist, in most cases they mainly differ in the size of their leaves. Particularly well suited for bonsai are the *Ficus benjamina exotica* and the *Ficus benjamina* 'Natascha,' both of which thrive with low light. As with most *Ficus* species, they tolerate an indoor climate well throughout the year and are easy to shape into beautiful bonsai forms.

Location: Like all other *Ficus* trees, this plant can be kept indoors throughout the year with no problem; during the winter months, it can even be kept near or above a radiator on a windowsill, because it loves having "warm feet." However, the plant also does well outside by mid spring in full sunlight or partial shade. Outside, the tree will become stronger and more compact. As soon as temperatures fall below 60°F (16°C), bring the plant back inside to a bright location and provide temperatures between 59 and 75°F (15 and 24°C). The tree will lose many leaves if kept in a place that is too dark. When exposed to high humidity with warm temperatures (e.g., in a warm winter garden or a small greenhouse) it will develop air roots, which will add to its interesting character.

Watering: As with all plants with leathery leaves and little evaporation, this tree needs little water. The soil should become somewhat dry before watering again. The cooler the temperature, the less watering is required. If the plant is overwatered, it sheds its leaves and the roots begin to rot.

Feeding: Use liquid bonsai fertilizer every 14 days from spring to fall. During the winter months, use it every four to six weeks, but only when the plant is in a warm location.

Transplanting: The best time for transplanting is spring, every 2 years; include root pruning. Provide good drainage.

Soil: Use either bonsai soil or loam–peat moss–sand in the ratio of 1:2:1.

Pruning: The branches can be pruned throughout the year. The white sap on the cut surface helps to heal the wound and is no reason for concern. Always shorten new shoots to 2 to 3 leaves after they have produced approximately 6 to 8 leaves. Leaf pruning is also well tolerated by this tree; however, it should be done only during the main growing season. In any case, leaves that have become too large should always be removed.

Wiring: Wiring is possible throughout the year, but only on branches that have lignified. Make sure that the wire is removed in time—after 3 to 6 months, depending on the growth.

Propagation: With cuttings during summer, or by air layering on a large plant in mid spring. It also is possible to use seeds.

Fortunella hindsii
Kumquat
Family: Rutaceae
Subtropics

Fortunella hindsii
Kumquat

The number of different species within the Rutaceae family is vast. They originally came from southeast Asia, but today are found in most subtropical climate zones. Their fruit are well known to all of us: oranges, lemons, kumquats, mandarin oranges, clementines, etc. The flowers of these little trees are white and have a strong scent. The bark of the plant is smooth and almost brownish green with whitish stripes, which adds to its charm. For a bonsai plant, choose only those with small leaves and fruit, to achieve proper proportions. The following are recommended: *Fortunella hindsii, Fortunella margarita, Fortunella japonica, Citrus mitis, Citrus aurantifolia,* and *Citrus microcarpa.*

Location: From the middle of spring (after the last frost), a partially shaded to sunny spot outdoors is ideal. By the end of summer, bring the plant back inside, where temperatures should not exceed 54°F (12°C), otherwise the plant will not get the rest it needs, and it will be weakened. Another consequence is the loss of leaves. If the plant remains indoors all year long, it needs much light and fresh air.

Watering: Keep the plant uniformly moist (not wet), and, if possible, use softened water. Good drainage is important to prevent "wet feet" and subsequent root rot.

Feeding: Use liquid bonsai fertilizer every 2 weeks during the main growing period, from spring through summer. Do not feed after that. Plan on one application of pulverized organic fertilizer in early summer.

Transplanting: Every 2–3 years, including root pruning. Do not place plant too far down into the soil. The neck of the root system should be above ground in order to prevent root rot.

Soil: Use either bonsai soil or loam, peat moss, and sand at a ratio of 2:1:1. Most citrus species love soil with a pH value of 5.0.

Pruning: Branches can be removed throughout the year. Be careful when pruning; if it is done too vigorously, particularly when only a limited amount of leaves are present, the tree will have difficulty producing new shoots. In addition, the formation of flower buds will be hindered. Large cut surfaces of branches should be covered with wound dressing material.

Wiring: Branches can be wired throughout the year, except when the plant is in bloom or when fruit is present. Shoots should be wired only after they have become lignified.

Propagation: By seed, cuttings, or grafting.

Fraxinus uhdei
Evergreen ash
Family: Oleaceae
Subtropics

Fraxinus uhdei
Evergreen ash

This evergreen grows about 49 feet tall (15 m) and has widespread, slightly drooping branches and an ash-grey bark. The pinnate leaves are about 4 inches (10 cm) long and deep green, with 5 to 9 small, lancet-shaped, featherlike leaflets. The leaflets are finely serrated with little teeth that are almost invisible to the naked eye. As a bonsai plant, the evergreen ash is most often found in Taiwan. This plant is robust and loves a lot of light, but will also tolerate places with less light. The relatively wide space between leaves can easily be remedied if, after the basic plant shape has been established, it is regularly cut back and the large leaves are removed.

Location: Indoors at a window; the more light, the more compact the plant will be. From mid spring through summer, it can also be kept in a partially sunny to sunny spot outdoors. During the winter, temperatures should be kept at about 60 to 68°F (16 to 20°C).

Watering: The frequency of watering influences the size of the leaves as well as the distance between them; therefore, let the soil become almost dry before watering.

Feeding: From early spring through summer, use liquid bonsai fertilizer every 2 weeks. The rest of the year, use it every 4 to 6 weeks.

Transplanting: Transplant every 2 years, in the spring; if a substantial root ball has been established, include vigorous root pruning.

Soil: Use either bonsai soil or loam, peat moss, and sand in a ratio of 1:1:1; if the amount of loam is increased, the plant will remain more compact.

Pruning: Can be done throughout the year, whenever it becomes necessary. Allow new shoots to become lignified and then shorten them to two or three leaves. All shoots that grow towards the inside should be removed. During the main growing period, continue to remove all large leaves.

Wiring: Wiring can be done whenever the branches have become lignified, from early fall on.

Propagation: With slightly hardened cuttings in early summer to mid summer in a peat moss–sand mixture at a 1:1 ratio; keep them at 68 to 77°F (20 to 25°C).

Gardenia jasminoides
Common gardenia
Family: Rubiaceae
Subtropics

Gardenia jasminoides
Common gardenia

This evergreen shrub from China grows anywhere from 3 to 26 feet tall (1 to 8 m), depending on species and origin, and is found from the tropics to the subtropics. The leaves are opposite, dark green, leathery, and shiny, and are a beautiful contrast to the waxlike, pure white to cream-colored flowers. The flowers are very fragrant and grow at the end of shoots; the main flowering period is from late winter to early spring. Gardenias are available as flowering houseplants throughout the year. In China, they are often cultivated in containers filled with water. In temperate regions, caring for a gardenia bonsai presents a few problems. A location that is too warm, soil kept too wet, or water that is too hard can lead to yellowing and subsequent loss of leaves and flower buds.

Location: This plant does well all year round indoors at a bright location, such as at a window, but not exposed to hot sun. During the winter months, temperatures should not fall below 53°F (12°C), and the plant should be watered sparingly. Optimal temperatures are between 59 and 64°F (15 and 18°C). Gardenias should not be allowed to get "cold, wet feet." Also, they need to be protected from dry air; do not place them above or near a heat source during the winter months. During the summer, the plants can be placed outside in a partially shaded area.

Watering: Use soft water (watering with mineral water is also suitable). Keep the soil uniformly moist. The rule of thumb for winter is: the colder the plant is kept, the less water it needs. If the soil is too wet, leaves and flowers will turn yellow and fall off.

Feeding: Use liquid bonsai fertilizer every 2 weeks from spring to fall.

Transplanting: In the spring, after flowering time, every 2 years, depending on growth; include root pruning. Provide good drainage to avoid root rot.

Soil: Use either bonsai soil or loam, peat moss, and sand at a ratio of 1:3:2.

Pruning: After the plant has flowered, cut back into the old woody part of the branches. Then let them grow if the plant is to bloom. If not, cut back the shoots continuously to 2 to 3 leaf pairs whenever the shoots have developed 6 pairs of leaves.

Wiring: Shaping the plant should start early, when it is still young, because it is easiest at that time. Remember to remove wire before damage occurs. The best time for wiring is right after the plant has stopped blooming, or when the new shoots have ripened.

Propagation: With cuttings (mid to late summer); warm soil encourages the development of roots.

Haematoxylum campechianum
Logwood tree
Family: Leguminosae
Tropics

Haematoxylum campechianum
Logwood

The logwood tree probably originated in the West Indies. It is a thorny bush, 20 to 26 feet tall (6 to 8 m), with gnarled branches and small, shiny, featherlike leaves that fold up at dusk. Its yellowish white flowers are inconspicuous, growing from the woody leaf axis. If the bark, or a thick branch, is removed from the trunk, a blood-red liquid appears, which turns a deep black as it is exposed to the air, which is why the *Haematoxylum* is called the *Blutholz (blood tree)* or *Tintenbaum (ink tree)* in German. New shoots are fiery red as long as the plant is outdoors and in full sunlight. The thorns grow on the leaf axil or on the left and right side of the petioles. All in all, it is a very interesting tree, which needs a great deal of light and, in the winter, temperatures above 59°F (15°C).

Location: The plant should be kept indoors at 59 to 71°F (15 to 22°C) in a very bright location. During the winter, temperatures shouldn't be less than 59°F (15°C). It may be placed outdoors in a sunny location from mid spring through summer.

Watering: In general, keep the soil uniformly moist at all times. If the plant is placed in a cooler location during the winter months, reduce watering; under all circumstances, avoid "wet feet."

Feeding: Use liquid bonsai fertilizer every 2 weeks from mid-spring through summer. In the fall and winter months, use it only every 4 weeks.

Transplanting: Transplant and prune the roots in the spring every two years.

Soil: Use either bonsai soil or loam, peat moss, and sand at a ratio of 1:1:1.

Pruning: Thick branches are best cut in early spring; new shoots, after they have developed 8 to 10 leaves, are cut back to 1 to 2 leaves.

Wiring: Wire shortly before the main growth period sets in (early spring) or in early fall, when new shoots are long enough and slightly lignified. Remove the wire in time to avoid scarring of the bark.

Propagation: With cuttings in early summer; temperatures around 77 to 86°F (25 to 30°C) are necessary for roots to develop. Propagation can also be accomplished with seeds; however, seed is not readily available.

Jacaranda mimosifolia
Jacaranda
Family: Bignoniaceae
Subtropics

Jacaranda mimosifolia
Jacaranda

The jacaranda is a semi-evergreen tree from Brazil, where it grows to an astounding height with a wide crown. Its leaves are fernlike and about 17½ inches long (45 cm), and its beautiful lavender-blue flowers face almost upright.

This tree can be found today in many subtropical regions (Tenerife, southern Spain, South America, North America, etc.). The large, feathery leaves present the greatest challenge to the bonsai gardener. But when the plant is in the right location, and with the proper pruning, watering, and feeding, the leaves can be reduced to 2¼ to 3 inches (6 to 8 cm); the feathering also becomes much more delicate.

Location: If the jacaranda is kept indoors throughout the year, it will be difficult to keep its leaves small. The plant does well in a very sunny spot, with lots of fresh air and, during the winter months, temperatures not below 53°F (12°C). If it doesn't have sufficient light, which will be the case in certain regions in the winter, the plant will shed its leaves, but then will grow them anew in the spring. In mid spring, try to place it in a partially shaded spot outside. During the winter, keep it indoors, between 53 and 71°F (12 and 22°C).

Watering: It is best to keep the soil uniformly moist throughout the year. Too much water will cause the leaves to turn yellow and drop off. If the root ball dries out, the leaves will shrink and turn brown. In order to keep the leaves small, water only enough to keep the leaves from rolling up and becoming brown.

Feeding: Use liquid bonsai fertilizer every two weeks from spring to fall; during the winter months, use it only when the plant has developed new shoots and is in a warm location.

Transplanting: Vigorously prune the roots and transplant every year in the spring, which will reduce the size of the leaves.

Soil: Use either bonsai soil or loam, peat moss, and sand at a ratio of 2:2:1.

Pruning: Shorten new shoots to 1 to 2 pairs of leaves, after they have produced at least 4 to 5 pairs. In addition, regularly remove all large leaves during the main growing period, keeping only those that are small. If two new shoots appear at the leaf axil, remove the one that seems to grow towards the inside. This way, the other develops into a branch that grows outward, keeping the crown from becoming too dense.

Wiring: Wiring can be done any time. Wiring is necessary with this plant to achieve a good form. Young shoots are wired only until they start to lignify.

Propagation: Grow from seeds. Since jacaranda seeds have a limited life, use the seeds immediately. Cover them with sand, and keep them uniformly moist at a temperature of at least 77°F (25°C).

Lagerstroemia indica
Crape myrtle
Family: Lythraceae
Subtropics

Lagerstroemia indica
Crape myrtle

The crape myrtle is a deciduous tree that grows as tall as 26 feet (8 m) in its native habitat. Its elliptical leaves are approximately 1 inch long (2.5 cm). In a sunny location, new shoots turn reddish in color, increasing the beauty of the plant. The flowers are produced in summer, appearing at the end of one-year-old shoots in panicles, in colors ranging from violet to pinkish red. The trunk has a brownish, smooth bark; as the tree gets older, the bark turns a faint pinkish color. The following two species also do well as bonsai: *Lagerstroemia hirsuta* (India to New Guinea), flowers are either purplish red or white; *Lagerstroemia speciosa* (India to Australia), 8 inches tall (20 cm), with pink to red flowers. Both come from the tropics and need warm locations.

Since *Lagerstroemia* needs a lot of sunlight and warm temperatures to produce its flowers, gardeners in temperate regions are only successful in bringing it into bloom when their summers are warm. If they are cool with lots of rain, the plant will not produce flowers and will be subject to mildew.

Location: The plant can only thrive indoors all year round in a sunny and well-ventilated area (winter garden). It is best to bring the plant outside in spring, after the last frost, to a sunny, warm spot. In the fall, before the first frost, keep the plant inside at temperatures between 43 and 50°F (6 and 10°C) in a coldhouse. The tropical varieties need temperatures between 50 and 59°F (10 and 15°C).

Watering: Water generously during the summer months; however, allow the soil to become partially dry between waterings. Water sparingly during the winter months, but don't let the soil dry out completely. From mid summer on, just before buds begin to form, reduce watering; this encourages bud formation.

Feeding: Use liquid bonsai fertilizer every 2 weeks from spring through fall; do not feed during the winter months.

Transplanting: It's best to transplant every two years in the spring, shortly before the development of new shoots; include root pruning. Make sure that the new container is not too large.

Soil: Use either bonsai soil or loam, peat moss, and sand at a ratio of 1:2:1.

Pruning: Whenever a new shoot has developed 6 leaves, cut it back to 1 to 2 leaves. This is important for shaping of the young tree, if you don't particularly want the tree to produce flowers. If you want flowers, do not prune before fall, or prune when the tree is finished blooming, or in the spring before new shoots have developed. Then cut back vigorously, leaving only one leaf bud on each one-year-old shoot, or pruning up to and into the lignified stems.

Wiring: Since young shoots of the *Lagerstroemia* become lignified very quickly and then are rather brittle, they should not be wired. Wiring may be done without negative effects only when the shoots are as thick as a pencil, but not beyond that point. Besides, this plant can easily be shaped through proper pruning.

Propagation: Use seed (in spring) or cuttings (from early summer on).

Lantana camara
Yellow sage
Family: Verbenaceae
Tropics

Lantana camara
Yellow sage

A small, colorful bush, the *Lantana camara* originally came from the West Indies, where it can still be found in many gardens and parks. Its flowers change their colors during the blooming season in the summer from pink, to red, to orange, and produce blue-black berries. The leaves, flowers, and roots have a very strong scent. This is a favorite plant of the whitefly. That aside, this plant is very undemanding and can easily tolerate vigorous pruning.

Location: Place the plant outside during the summer months, in full sunlight and fresh air. During the winter months, the plant needs temperatures between 41 and 46°F (5 and 8°C), but it will tolerate a warmer location.

Watering: Water generously during the summer months; water sparingly in the winter, but not so little that the root ball dries out.

Feeding: Use liquid bonsai fertilizer every two weeks in the fall. Do not feed during the winter months if the plant is kept in a cold location.

Transplanting: Every 2 years in the spring; include root pruning.

Soil: Use either bonsai soil or loam, peat moss, and sand in a ratio of 1:1:1; add a little powdered organic fertilizer to the soil (1 teaspoon for a bowl 6 inches [15 cm] in diameter).

Pruning: Reduce shoots after the blooming is completed to 1 pair of leaves. This may be done at any time of year that the shoots are long enough. Cut large leaves off continuously during the main growing period.

Wiring: Caution! The branches on this plant are very brittle. Be careful when wiring—and only do so if you think it is necessary.

Propagation: Use either cuttings or seed.

Malpighia coccigera
Miniature holly
Family: Malpighiaceae
Subtropics

Malpighia coccigera
Miniature holly

A 3-foot-tall (1 m) bush, with shiny green, thorny leaves, small light-pink flowers, and red, pea-sized fruit. The flowers usually grow from the leaf axils on lignified twigs. The main flowering period in temperate regions is in the spring and summer. This bush is also known as Singapore holly and Japanese holly. The *Malpighia glabra* (Barbados cherry), which has somewhat larger leaves, flowers, and fruits, can also be transformed into a bonsai. In contrast to the *Malpighia coccigera*, whose leaves have sharp points on the edges, the leaves of the *Malpighia glabra* are oval and smooth. Whenever the plant is moved to another spot or experiences temperature changes, it tends to shed its leaves; however, they grow back rather quickly.

Location: Can be kept indoors all year at a bright window. Do not let the temperature during the winter months go below 57°F (14°C); otherwise, the plant will lose its leaves. A very bright location with temperatures between 64 and 75°F (18 and 24°C) is ideal. The plant can also be placed outdoors in a sunny to partly sunny location in mid spring, but it needs to be protected from high noon sun.

Watering: This plant needs a great deal of water. It is best to keep the soil uniformly moist. If the root ball is allowed to dry out, the plant will lose its leaves.

Feeding: Use liquid bonsai fertilizer once every week, but, during the winter months, use it about every four weeks. This plant likes plenty of nitrogen. If its leaves turn yellow, give it an application of an iron supplement.

Transplanting: Every 1 to 2 years in the spring; include vigorous root pruning, because the roots grow very fast and need a lot of soil. Don't choose a container much larger than the previous one.

Soil: Use either bonsai soil or loam, peat moss, and sand at a ratio of 2:1:1.

Pruning: Pruning can be done throughout the year when branches become lignified; when shoots have developed 5 to 6 pairs of leaves, cut back to 1 to 2 pairs of leaves. Remove all small leaves that are growing inside the crown, on the trunk and the branches. The best time to prune this plant to its basic form is just before the onset of the main growing season.

Wiring: Wiring can be done throughout the year, whenever the branches become lignified. Thick branches are difficult to bend, and they tear easily; therefore, establish the basic form when the plant is still young.

Propagation: From mid spring through summer, with cuttings; they need warm soil in order to develop roots. Propagation is also possible by seeds; however, seeds are not readily available.

Murraya paniculata
Orange jasmine
Family: Rutaceae
Tropics

Murraya paniculata
Orange jasmine

In its tropical habitat of southern China, India, and Indonesia, this evergreen tree, with its alternate, feathery leaves, is called the "cosmetic bark tree," since its bark is used in the manufacture of cosmetics. The tree has heavily scented flowers, similar to those of citrus trees. It produces red berries that fall down to the soil when ripe and sprout easily. The tree has a strong, old-looking trunk with grayish beige, smooth bark. Southern China and Taiwan, where most of the orange jasmine bonsai trees come from, have many very beautiful, very old specimens.

Location: This plant can be kept inside throughout the year near a bright window, with temperatures between 61 and 71°F (16 and 22°C); during the winter months, the temperatures should not fall below 59°F (15°C). The tree also does well in a sunny to partially shaded location outdoors during the summer months. If placed in full sunlight, it will grow smaller leaves and become very compact; however, the leaves will turn slightly yellow.

Watering: Water generously during the main growing period. However, if the plant is kept in a cool location during the winter months, keep temperatures between 59 and 64°F (15 and 18°C) and let the soil become partially dry before watering.

Feeding: Use liquid bonsai fertilizer every 2 weeks from early spring through summer. Feed only every 4 to 6 weeks in the winter, but only if the plant is in a spot where the temperature is above 64°F (18°C) and it is growing well.

Transplanting: Repot in the spring, but only when a substantial root system has developed; include vigorous root pruning.

Soil: Use either bonsai soil or loam, peat moss, and sand at a ratio of 2:2:1.

Wiring: Wiring can be done throughout the year; however, wire young shoots only after they have become lignified. Thick branches are difficult to bend; begin shaping the tree when the branches are the thickness of a pencil.

Pruning: The branches can be pruned all year. Cut new shoots back to two or three leaves after six leaves have developed on each shoot, or when the portion of the branch has begun to lignify. Large, old leaves should also be removed at this time. Since flower buds begin to appear usually in early summer, always on the tips of shoots, take this into consideration if you want your tree to flower.

Propagation: Use seed or cuttings. Seeds should be removed from the pulp of the red fruit and then sown immediately. Cuttings can be used from mid summer on; plant them in soil at approximately 82°F (28°C) soil temperature.

Myrciaria cauliflora
Jaboticaba
Family: Myrtaceae
Subtropics and tropics

Myrciaria cauliflora
Jaboticaba

The jaboticaba comes from Brazil, where it is a very popular fruit tree, reaching a height of 50 to 53 feet (10 to 12 m). The tree can be found from Colombia, through Paraguay, to Argentina, and occasionally in Florida. The branching on this tree begins just above the ground; the bark is smooth and usually speckled in shades of brown and grey. Its bright green, oval-shaped leaves are slightly pink right after they open, if sufficient light is available. White flowers appear directly on the trunk and branches, and grow into large, shiny, brownish red, cherrylike fruit. Inside the white-colored flesh of the fruit are 1 to 4 small seeds, which germinate easily if they are sown immediately. In their native habitat, people love to eat the slightly sour tasting fruit fresh, or use them to make a marmalade.

Location: This plant can be kept indoors all year at a bright window, or outside from mid spring through summer in a sunny or slightly shaded spot. In winter, keep temperatures between 61 and 75°F (16 and 24°C).

Watering: Water generously during the summer months; sparsely in winter. It is best to keep the soil uniformly moist.

Feeding: Use liquid fertilizer every 14 days from early spring through summer; this plant does not like highly concentrated fertilizer.

Transplanting: The best time for transplanting is every 2 years in the spring; include moderate root pruning.

Soil: Use either bonsai soil or loam, peat moss, and sand at a ratio of 1:2:2.

Pruning: Shorten shoots to 2 to 4 pairs of leaves after 6 to 8 pairs of leaves have developed. Vigorous pruning or removal of branches is possible throughout the year, but the best time is in the spring.

Wiring: Since the plant naturally grows like a tree, wiring is seldom necessary; if wiring is done, wrap only lignified branches.

Propagation: With seeds from the jaboticaba fruit, or with cuttings from mid summer on.

Myrtus communis
Myrtle
Family: Myrtaceae
Subtropics

Myrtus communis
Myrtle

The *Myrtus communis*, already known in ancient times, is a small evergreen tree with little, dark green leaves and white flowers that grow from the leaf axil in summer. Its habitat is the Mediterranean area, where it reaches 16 feet (5 m) in height, even in very poor soil. The flowers develop into round, blue-black berries that are about the size of a pea. They are edible and are used to this day as a spice. The myrtle is a shrub with many symbolic associations; it is shrouded in legend. Its branches, made into a wreath, still adorn brides on their wedding day. The tree has been used since the 17th century as a houseplant and was one of the plants most often found in the houses of the middle classes. The age of central heating, which brought with it dry air and high temperatures, caused this charming houseplant to disappear slowly, because it didn't do well in such an environment. Not until recently—when we began to cut back on heating and save energy, and rediscovered the winter garden—did this plant come back into vogue. As a bonsai, it is highly recommended, since it grows well and is easy to shape.

Location: The myrtle can be kept indoors in a very bright, airy location. During the winter months it needs a bright but cool place, with temperatures between about 39 and 50°F (4 and 10°C), but under no circumstances too close to a heating source. If the plant is placed in a warmer location, lower the nighttime temperature and make sure that it gets plenty of fresh air. The plant can also be outside from the mid spring through summer, in a slightly sunny to partially shaded location.

Watering: Water generously (with soft water) during the main growing season and the height of summer, but sparingly during the winter months. Try to avoid letting the root ball dry out and avoid "wet feet." A basic rule: keep soil evenly moist.

Feeding: Use liquid bonsai fertilizer every two weeks from spring to the end of summer. If the plant is placed in a cool spot during the winter months—between 39 and 59°F (4 and 15°C)—discontinue feeding. When the temperature is between 61 and 64°F (16 and 18°C), feed twice during the winter.

Transplanting: Repot about every 2 years; younger plants, every 3 to 5 years. With older plants, only repot when the soil is almost used up. Provide good drainage and prune the roots lightly when transplanting.

Soil: Use either bonsai soil or loam, peat moss, and sand at a ratio of 1:1:2.

Pruning: Shorten new shoots to two to three leaves after the twigs have become lignified. If you want the plant to bloom, don't prune from the early spring until the plant has stopped blooming.

Wiring: The best time for wiring is in spring, or after the plant has finished blooming; only wire lignified branches.

Propagation: With cuttings throughout the year, or use seeds immediately after harvesting the berries—but first remove the fruit pulp.

Olea europaea
Common olive
Family: Oleaceae
Subtropics

Olea europaea
Common olive

The olive tree has always been an important part of the culture of the Mediterranean region as well as being a medicinal plant. Its fruit has yielded olive oil; its wood was used for building and for lathe work. To this day, the olive is a delicacy and is prized the world over. The tree itself lives a very long time, and, when it is old, has a fissured bark that resembles a bizarrely shaped rock. The tree has oblong, silvery-green, leathery leaves and whitish yellow flowers in the leaf axils. Depending on the variety, the tree produces green or bluish black olives, which are ready for harvest by late summer or early fall.

Location: The olive tree can be kept indoors throughout the year at a bright, sunny window, or outside, in a sunny area, after mid spring. During the winter months, keep the plant in a light, airy spot. Ideal temperatures are between 43 and 53°F (6 and 12°C), but higher temperatures are also possible—up to 64°F (18°C); however, if the plant is in a warmer spot, lower the nighttime temperatures.

Watering: During the summer as well as the winter, let the soil dry out partially, and then water generously. Water more often when the tree is kept in a brighter and warmer location.

Feeding: Use liquid bonsai fertilizer every two weeks from spring through summer. In addition, apply pulverized organic fertilizer once in mid spring, sprinkling it on top of the soil (1 teaspoon for a 6-inch-wide [15 cm] bowl).

Transplanting: Repot every two years in spring; include root pruning.

Soil: Use either bonsai soil or loam, peat moss, and sand at a ratio of 2:1:1.

Pruning: Cut back branches all year round, but not too drastically, because it is difficult for small olive trees to produce new shoots. Let new shoots grow until they have eight pairs of leaves and then shorten them to two pairs or let new shoots grow longer and then wire them for shaping when they become lignified.

Wiring: Branches can be wired throughout the year; shoots, when they become lignified. Start shaping when the plant is still young, since only relatively thin branches can be bent easily.

Propagation: With cuttings that are half-ripe during summer; plant them in a warm location. The easiest way is to let cuttings first take root in a glass of water. Another method is with seeds (olive pits) at 68°F (20°C).

Pistacia lentiscus
Mastic tree
Family: Anarcardiaceae
Subtropics

Pistacia lentiscus
Mastic tree

The mastic tree probably originated in central Asia, but it has been known for many thousands of years in the Middle East and the eastern Mediterranean region—particularly for its fruit, the pistachio nut. The mastic tree is an evergreen tree that reaches up to 33 feet (10 m) in height, has grey-green, feathery leaves. From the leaf axils, inconspicuous brownish green racemes grow. The fruit is 1¼ inches long (3 cm) and usually three-sided; inside the shell lies the light green pistachio nut. The plant is dioecious, which means that the male and female blossoms are on separate plants, so you need both to produce fruit. Caring for a *Pistacia* bonsai is very simple; the small tree makes few demands. Wiring is somewhat more difficult, since the branches grow very straight.

Location: During the summer months, the best location outdoors is in full sunlight, because then the plant will produce beautiful new shoots that are reddish in color; however, the plant will also tolerate partial shade. When temperatures reach 53°F (12°C) in the fall, bring the plant back inside and place it in a bright window, with temperatures between 50 and 53°F (10 and 12°C), although warmer temperatures (53 to 64°F [12 to 18°C]) are also suitable. If temperatures fall below 50°F (10°C), the tree will shed its leaves, go into a dormant period, and begin to grow leaves again in the spring.

Watering: The mastic tree, like all trees with leathery leaves, does not require much water; let the soil dry out partially before watering it, or before immersing it in a water bath. During the winter months, if the plant is in a cool location, barely water it at all and then only enough to prevent it from drying out.

Feeding: Use liquid bonsai fertilizer every two to four weeks from spring through summer; do not fertilize during the winter months.

Transplanting: Repot every two years in the spring; include root pruning. If the container is too small, you will limit the amount of soil; growth will be weak and shoots will be shorter.

Soil: Bonsai soil is preferred; or use loam, peat moss, and sand at a ratio of 1:1:1.

Pruning: The branches are best pruned during the main growing season. New shoots should grow 6 to 8 leaves, and then be cut back to 2 to 3 leaves. Regularly remove leaves growing on the lower parts of the branches.

Propagation: Use either pistachio nuts or cuttings. (Remember: roasted nuts won't germinate!) Plant ripened cuttings in early summer.

Podocarpus macrophyllus 'Maki'
Southern yew
Family: Podocarpaceae
Subtropics

Podocarpus macrophyllus 'Maki'
Southern yew

Podocarpus macrophyllus is called the "pine of the Buddhists" in China and Japan. This tree grows to about 33 to 49 feet tall (10 to 15 m) and has dark green, yewlike needles. The female flowers grow upright and look like willow catkins; the berries are bluish purple.

In contrast to the above-mentioned species, the *Podocarpus macrophyllus* 'Maki' cultivar can usually be found only in China, where the tree is called the "China yew." The tree is more compact, its needles are considerably shorter, and the oval-shaped, fleshy fruit are bluish green to purple-red. The tree is a conifer and does well as a bonsai plant. In addition, it is very robust and thrives with less light.

Location: Keep the plant indoors at a bright window, although it will also tolerate a darker location. Keep temperatures during the winter months between 61 and 68°F (16 and 20°C), and, if possible, not over a heat source. In spring after the danger of frost is over, take the plant outside to a partially sunny location.

Watering: Since the small, leathery leaves don't lose much moisture by transpiration, water sparingly, but do not let the root ball dry out.

Feeding: Use liquid bonsai fertilizer every two weeks from spring to fall; use it every four to six weeks during the winter months.

Transplanting: Every 2 to 3 years, in the spring; include root pruning if the root system has become very dense.

Soil: Use either bonsai soil or loam, peat moss, and sand at a ratio of 1:1:1.

Pruning: Pruning and shaping are possible throughout the year. Cut new shoots back to ¾ inch to 1½ inches (2 to 4 cm), after they have grown to about 2½ to 4 inches (6 to 10 cm).

Wiring:
After the shoots become lignified in late summer, they can be wired. Cushion-shaped branch groupings can be developed in following years. Try not to trap needles under the wires.

Propagation: With seed, or with ripe cuttings in mid to late summer.

Portulacaria afra
Elephant bush
Family: Portulacaceae
Dry subtropics

Portulacaria afra
Elephant bush

The Portulacaceae originate in the dry regions of South Africa. They are succulent plants, which means that their fleshy stems, branches, and leaves are able to store water for a long time. The elephant bush grows to about 10 feet tall (3 m). It has thick, almost round leaves about ¾ inch wide (2 cm) and delicate light pink flowers. It is a very undemanding plant, which is particularly well suited for gardeners who travel often or, for other reasons, have difficulty watering. This plant can manage to be without water for up to four weeks without suffering any ill effects. Shaping is also easy; in other words, it is an ideal plant for the beginner.

Location: The elephant bush can be kept indoors throughout the year at a bright window. It needs a lot of fresh air in the summer. As soon as possible after the last frost, bring the plant outside to a spot where it will receive full sunlight; partial shade is also suitable. If the plant is placed in full sunlight, the leaves will remain small and the shoots, compact. The best temperature range during the winter months is between 50 and 61°F (10 and 16°C), but between 61 and 71°F (16 and 22°C) also is tolerated. However, when the latter is the case, nighttime temperatures must be lowered.

Watering: Water only after the soil is quite dry; this plant needs little water. If it is placed in a cool location during the winter months, water only every four to eight weeks.

Feeding: Use liquid bonsai fertilizer every four weeks from spring through summer; do not fertilize during the winter months.

Transplanting: Repot and prune the roots every two years. Late spring is ideal, but anytime is alright.

Soil: Use either bonsai soil or loam, peat moss, and sand at a ratio of 2:1:2.

Pruning: Branches from early spring through summer; new shoots at any time. Cut back to 1 or 2 pairs of leaves after 4 or 5 leaf pairs have developed (near the end of summer). To create a clean-looking shape, always remove all shoots that grow directly on the trunk, or branches that grow inside the crown.

Wiring: The best time is from the middle to the end of summer; proceed carefully, since the bark is sensitive and branches tend to break off easily.

Propagation: Cuttings work well. Make cuttings about 2½ to 6 inches long (6 to 15 cm); let them dry out for two weeks; and then plant them in a dry peat moss–sand mixture. Do not water until small root fibres have developed.

Psidium guajava
Common guava
Family: Myrtaceae
Tropics

Psidium guajava
Common guava

The common or apple guava, originally from the tropical zones of the Americas, is found today in almost all warm regions. The tree grows to about 26 feet tall (8 m) and has a light to dark green bark; it sheds small pieces of bark continuously. Its young shoots are four-sided. It has opposite, oval leaves that have a downy covering on the underside, and it produces white flowers from the leaf axils. The pear-shaped fruit is about 1½ to 4 inches long (4 to 10 cm) and rich in vitamins A and C. The fruit is ideal for making marmalade and juice.

Location: During the summer months, keep the guava outside in a sunny and warm place (no drafts); or indoors in a spot that is as bright as possible. During the winter months, keep it in a bright location and in temperatures ranging from about 53 to 64°F (12 to 18°C).

Watering: Keep the soil uniformly moist during the growing period. Since this bonsai keeps its leaves during the winter, it needs some water during this time of year. However, remember: the cooler the location, the less water is required. Avoid "wet feet."

Feeding: Use bonsai fertilizer once a month during the growing period. Do not fertilize during the winter months.

Transplanting: Repot every two years in early spring, or when the plant starts to show new growth.

Soil: Use either bonsai soil or loam, peat moss, and sand at a ratio of 1:3:1. The soil needs to be porous in order to let water run through it, to prevent "wet feet."

Pruning: The branches should be pruned before new growth begins. With a young plant, prune new shoots when they have developed 5 pairs of leaves, cutting back to 2 to 3 pairs. With older plants, cut back continuously to 1 pair of leaves after 3 pairs have developed on a shoot. If the plant grows vigorously, the largest leaves can also be cut off.

Wiring: If wiring is necessary, do so only when shoots have become lignified.

Propagation: Use either seeds or cuttings at 77°F (25°C). Seeds sprout in three weeks.

Punica granatum 'Nana'
Dwarf pomegranate
Family: Punicaceae
Subtropics

Punica granatum 'Nana'
Dwarf pomegranate

This tree already was known in Egypt in 2500 B.C. The pomegranate also was mentioned several times in the Old Testament. It can be found today in all subtropical regions, and occasionally in tropical regions. Two varieties, *Punica granatum* and *Punica granatum* 'Nana,' are ideal for bonsai. The latter is the smallest variety, growing to about 5 feet (1.5 m) tall. It is richly branched, with small, myrtlelike, bright green leaves, which the plant sheds during the winter season, and orange-red flowers that appear in the summer at the tips of new shoots. It bears the famous pomegranate, a sour fruit. If your bonsai *Punica* bears many fruit, leave only 2 or 3 on the tree; otherwise the tree will become too weak.

Location: If the plant is kept indoors during the summer, it must be in a bright, airy spot. During the winter months, keep it in a cool place (a staircase or unheated room), with temperatures around 43 to 50°F (6 to 10°C), or even lower. If the plant is not allowed to rest and is kept too warm, its new shoots will be thin and weak. What would be ideal is a sunny location from mid spring on outdoors; after the tree has shed its leaves in the fall, bring it indoors again.

Watering: Water generously during the summer, but always make sure that the soil is partially dry before watering. During the winter, if the plant is in a cool location (43 to 50°F [6 to 10°C]), reduce watering, but don't allow the root ball to dry out completely.

Feeding: Use liquid bonsai fertilizer every two weeks from spring to the end of summer. Do not feed the plant during its dormant season, unless it is in a warm place; then feed it every six weeks.

Transplanting: Repot every two years in the spring, before new growth begins. Include root pruning, but only if the root system is well developed.

Soil: Use either bonsai soil or loam, peat moss, and sand in a ratio of 1:1:1.

Pruning: The pomegranate can be pruned throughout the year. Prune new shoots after 8 to 10 pairs of leaves have developed, cutting back to 1 to 3 pairs of leaves. Continuously remove all shoots that grow straight up or towards the inside of the crown in order to achieve a clear form. Note: if you want the tree to bloom, do not prune shoots after the start of spring.

Wiring: Wrap only those branches that are about half as thick as a pencil. The best time is after the plant has finished blooming or before new growth sets in.

Propagation: Use seeds or cuttings. Seeds should be soaked in water for 24 hours prior to sowing. Place them on top of a peat moss—sand mixture and then cover them with a thick layer of the mixture, and keep them at a temperature of between 68 and 86°F (20 and 30°C). To propagate by cuttings, use unlignified cuttings from mid to late summer.

Rhododendron simsii
Sim's azalea
Family: Ericaceae
Subtropics

Rhododendron simsii
Sim's azalea

The azalea is native to the humid regions of southern China and along the Yangtze River. This huge genus is composed of hundreds of species that come in a wide array of colors, flowers, and shapes. We are familiar with the evergreen azalea, which usually blooms from fall to spring and is available in flower shops and nurseries. In China and Japan, this plant has had a long tradition as a bonsai plant. Indeed, clubs have formed there that have dedicated themselves exclusively to the creation of azalea bonsai.

Location: The best place, from the beginning of spring to just before the first frost, is a cool, somewhat sun-protected spot outdoors. After that, keep the plant indoors, in an airy, bright location in a winter garden at about 42 to 53°F (6 to 12°C). When its buds develop in winter, place it in a slightly warmer spot, with temperatures around 59 to 71°F (15 to 22°C). When the plant has finished blooming, it should be placed outside again. The azalea will thrive exclusively indoors only if it is provided with a great deal of fresh air and light, and temperatures are not too high.

Watering: Water generously during the summer, particularly when the plant is in bloom, with soft water (mineral water); during the rest of the year, keep it uniformly moist. The root ball of an azalea should never be allowed to dry out.

Feeding: After blooming is over, feed the plant every two weeks until late summer with organic acid-rich liquid fertilizer (made from peat moss). Do not feed the plant during the winter or while it is in bloom, except when it is "hungry," which is the case when the leaves turn yellow.

Transplanting: Repot and lightly prune the roots every two to three years after the plant has finished blooming. Make sure to provide good drainage when you repot.

Soil: Use bonsai soil and acid-containing peat moss mixed together in equal amounts, or use a mixture of loam, peat moss, and sand at a ratio of 1:4:2. But you can also buy a ready-made azalea soil (pH value of 4.5), which is available in nurseries or bonsai specialty shops.

Pruning: The branches can be pruned throughout the year. The green, freshly sprouting shoots that develop around the flower buds must be removed (pull down when picking them off), otherwise the buds will dry out. Also, remove wilted flowers. Wait until new shoots are about 1½ inches long (4 cm), and cut them back to the lignified portion. Buds develop at the ends of new shoots in the fall. If no flowers are desired, cut back all new shoots to 1 to 2 pairs of leaves as soon as 6 to 8 pairs have developed.

Wiring: The best time to wire is after blooming is finished; however, be careful when bending the branches, because they are very brittle.

Propagation: Use cuttings; however, this is relatively difficult. It's better to buy an azalea plant in the nursery and create your bonsai from it.

Rosmarinus officinalis
Rosemary
Family: Labiatae
Subtropics

Rosmarinus officinalis
Rosemary

This evergreen bush is at home in the Mediterranean countries, where it grows to a height of about 5 feet (1.5 m). Its needle-shaped, somewhat leathery, dark green leaves are silvery on the underside, very fragrant, and known to us as the herb *rosemary*. This shrub is difficult to grow indoors, so it is essential that it be placed outdoors during the summer. In its habitat it blooms almost all year. The flowers are light blue. The interesting, fibrous bark, which the plant sheds partially, makes this bonsai plant look very old, even when it is still young.

Location: When kept indoors, this plant should be in a bright spot, with temperatures between 41 and 46°F (5 and 8°C). It should be placed outdoors in full sunlight soon after the last frost.

Watering: Keep it on the dry side during the winter, but do not let the soil dry out completely. During the summer, water a bit more; but when the weather is cool, make sure that the soil doesn't get too wet, otherwise the plant will react by letting shoots—and often whole branches—die off.

Feeding: Discontinue feeding during the winter months. Starting in the spring and continuing through summer, feed every three weeks with liquid bonsai fertilizer.

Transplanting: Every 2 to 3 years, before new growth sets in; include root pruning.

Soil: Use either bonsai soil or loam, peat moss, and sand at a ratio of 1:1:2. Add 1 teaspoon of lime for each 8-inch-wide (20 cm) container.

Wiring: Since the branches of the rosemary are somewhat stiff, wiring is necessary in shaping them. However, the diameter of the branches should only be half that of a pencil, otherwise they will easily be broken when you try to wire them.

Pruning: The branches can be pruned throughout the year. New shoots should be cut back continuously to the desired length when they have reached 2 inches (5 cm) in length. The branches can be formed into beautiful cushion shapes by repeatedly reducing the shoots.

Propagation: This is best accomplished with cuttings in summer.

Sageretia theezans
Family: Rhamnaceae
Subtropics

Sageretia theezans

This shrub's home is in southern China, where, depending on the location, it may shed its leaves during the winter. The 6-foot-long (2 m) twisting branches develop spines. The shiny, bright green leaves are the size of a fingernail. The flowers are inconspicuous, with whitish petals that only develop if the shoots are not cut back. In the fall, the plant produces small green berries, which turn blackish blue when ripe. The bark is brown, but, the older the tree becomes, the more vividly speckled the bark becomes. This is an excellent plant to shape into a bonsai, because of its vigorous growth and because its trunk, branches, and leaves are optimally proportioned. The plant tolerates vigorous pruning and branches out beautifully. Mildew, yellowing leaves, and whitefly can be problems during the winter months, if there is a lack of fresh air and the temperatures are too high.

Location: Inside, in a bright, airy spot. During the winter, do not place the plant near a heat source. Ideal temperatures are between 53 and 64°F (12 and 18°C). However, this plant can also survive the winter at temperatures between 35 and 46°F (2 and 8°C); it will shed all or part of its leaves (dormant period), but it will grow new leaves in the spring. If it is kept in a spot with temperatures between 64 and 75°F (18 and 24°C), make sure that it receives sufficient fresh air and light.

Watering: Water generously during the growing period, particularly in the summer, but avoid "wet feet." During the winter months, allow the soil to become partially dry before watering again.

Feeding: Use liquid bonsai fertilizer every two weeks. However, during the winter months, use it only once a month and only if the plant is placed in a warm location.

Transplanting: Repotting is best done in the spring every 1 to 2 years, along with root pruning, provided the tree has developed a mature root system.

Soil: Use either bonsai soil or loam, peat moss, and sand at a ratio of 2:2:1.

Pruning: Pruning and shaping can be done throughout the year. Cut new shoots back to 2 to 3 leaves when they have become lignified, or when 12 leaves—or pairs of leaves—have developed.

Wiring: Always wire when branches and shoots have become lignified. Start shaping the plant early, because when its branches become too thick, they cannot be bent.

Propagation: Use cuttings in summer, or use seeds.

Schefflera arboricola
Family: Araliaceae
Subtropics

Schefflera arboricola

In contrast to the *Schefflera arboricola*, whose habitat is the subtropical regions, the *Schefflera actinophylla* (Australian umbrella tree) grows in the tropical regions. It has umbrellalike, palmate, long-stemmed leaves, which account for its name. The *S. actinophylla* grows to a height of 49 to 98 feet (15 to 30 m) in its native habitat and has beautiful, dense umbels with fleshy, wine-red flowers. The *Schefflera arboricola* is much smaller; its leaves are only 8 inches (20 cm) in diameter and are delicately divided. Its upright umbels produce orange-red to black berries. Both species do well as bonsai. They are very robust; it is difficult to kill them, unless you overwater. The trunk remains relatively thin and does not branch out into a crown, as some other tropical bushes do. The *Schefflera* is often cultivated as a rock bonsai, because it develops mangrovelike roots. If the trunk has grown to its desired size, the tips of the shoots can be removed, causing the plant to grow new shoots. Repeatedly pruning the shoots this way will increase branching, resulting in a more compact plant.

Location: Keep *Schefflera* inside at a very bright window, giving it as much light as possible; the more light the plant receives, the shorter the leaf stalks and the smaller the leaves. The ideal temperatures are between 64 and 71°F (18 and 22°C); temperatures should not be below 59°F (15°C). The *Schefflera* can also be placed close to a heat source. If the location is too dark, the *Schefflera* leaf stalks will become very long. The results of overwatering are very large leaves and possibly root rot. When the temperature in the spring reaches above 59°F (15°C), place the plant outside in full sun (allow the plant to get used to the outdoors slowly, however). In the autumn, when temperatures fall below 59°F (15°C), bring the plant back in.

Watering: In order to develop short internodes, small leaves, and keep the plant healthy, water as little as possible; however, don't allow the soil to dry out completely.

Feeding: Feed every four weeks with liquid bonsai fertilizer; too much nitrogen leads to large leaves.

Transplanting: Repot and vigorously prune the roots every two years; when transplanting, also remove all large leaves.

Soil: Use either bonsai soil or loam, peat moss, and sand at a ratio of 1:1:1.

Pruning: When new shoots have reached their desired length, remove their tips. At the same time, also remove large leaves; leave the leaf stalks in place, since they will fall off by themselves in about four weeks. Older trees will develop air roots, providing that the humidity is high enough, which increases their exotic appearance.

Wiring: Wiring is possible while the shoots are still somewhat green—in other words, not yet lignified; however, care must be taken that the wire does not injure the bark.

Propagation: Propagate by seed. Sow immediately after receiving the seeds, at a temperature of about 68 to 86°F (20 to 30°C). The seeds take only a short time to germinate. Cover the seeds with sand or soil.

Serissa foetida
Family: Rubiaceae
Subtropics

Serissa foetida

"Tree of 100 stars," or "June snow," or "shrub of strong scent"—these are the names of this plant in China. And the names are well-suited for this tree, which blooms so easily.

The main flowering season of the *Serissa* is in early spring; however, depending on the intensity of the light and the frequency of pruning, the plant may flower 2 to 3 times a year. The flowers come in a great variety of colors and shapes (pink and white, double and single, with petals that are serrated or smooth). The leaves are green with yellow veins and edges. An unmistakable characteristic of this evergreen shrub is the intense smell that is released when its roots or shoots are cut. That's why the plant is called *S. foetida*—which, in Latin, means "the smelly one." The flowers grow from the tips of the shoots whenever they have reached their maximum length. Blooming can be increased if the wilted flowers are not left on the stems, but are picked off immediately. The *Serissa* has a very interesting root system. We can make use of it by leaving the upper portion of the roots exposed.

Location: Place the plant indoors at a bright, airy window. Do not place it on top of a heating source during the winter, because it will lose its leaves. The temperature range is around 64 to 68°F (18 to 20°), but somewhat lower is even better. The plant can be kept outdoors, in a sunny or partially shaded spot, from mid spring through summer.

Watering: During the summer months when the weather is warm, the plant needs to be watered generously. But as a general rule, for summer as well as winter, keep the soil uniformly moist. Avoid keeping the plant with "wet feet," otherwise the fine root fibres will rot, which can result in the loss of leaves, and dead branches.

Feeding: Use liquid organic fertilizer every two weeks from late spring to fall; during the winter months, if the plant is kept in a warm place, use the fertilizer every 4 to 6 weeks.

Transplanting: Repot every two years and moderately prune the roots in early spring, before the growing season.

Soil: Use either bonsai soil or loam, peat moss, and sand at a ratio of 1:1:1.

Pruning: In general, prune branches and twigs any time it is necessary. Shorten new shoots to 1 to 2 pairs of leaves after they have developed 4 to 8 pairs of leaves. In order to keep the plant compact, it is necessary to prune back into the old, lignified portions. Make sure to remove all branches and twigs that grow straight upward or to the inside of the crown.

Wiring: Always done after the branches to be wired have become lignified. New shoots are wired whenever they have reached the desired length and are sufficiently lignified.

Propagation: Very easy with 4-inch-long (10 cm) cuttings in a glass of water from early summer on.

Tamarindus indica
Tamarind
Family: Leguminosae
Tropical rainforest

Tamarindus indica
Tamarind

The tamarind tree originally came from Africa. From there, it reached India, and later, Arabia and Persia. It is grown today in almost all tropical regions as a fruit and shade tree. It is an evergreen tree, which grows up to 82 feet tall (25 m), with a strong trunk and thin, rough bark. The light green, scented leaves are divided into 20 to 30 pairs of feathery leaflets; the leaves can be reduced in size relatively easily by the bonsai process. The beautiful, orchidlike flowers are yellowish with red markings; flowers develop on new shoots.

The brown legumes, about 2 to 7 inches (5 to 18 cm) long, have a mushy fruit pulp within which the seeds are embedded. In Arabia, the taste of the fruit pulp was compared to that of dried dates, and therefore called "Indian dates."

Location: Indoors throughout the year in a very bright location, since the plant needs a great deal of light. When the weather gets warm, it will do well in a sunny spot outside. In the fall, when the nights begin to get cooler, the plant should be taken inside and placed in a spot where the temperatures are between 59 and 68°F (15 and 20°C). If the plant is kept too cool or without sufficient light, it will shed its leaves, though they will grow again when it gets warmer.

Watering: Keep the plant uniformly moist during the summer. Reduce watering during the winter if it is kept in a cool place. Avoid giving the plant "wet feet."

Feeding: Use liquid bonsai fertilizer every four weeks from spring to summer. During the winter months, do not feed the plant if it is kept in a cool place.

Transplanting: The best time for transplanting is every two years in the spring, when the plant begins to develop new shoots, but it can also be done in the summer after the plant has been cut back. Do not forget to prune the roots at the same time.

Soil: Use either bonsai soil or loam, peat moss, and sand at a ratio of 1:1:1.

Pruning: As with most tropical bonsai, prune the tamarind tree during the main growing season (from spring through summer). If you want the branches that are developing new shoots to become thicker, let them grow until they have 10 to 12 leaves and then cut them back to 1 to 2 leaves. If you want the branches to develop normally, wait until 5 to 6 leaves have developed, and then shorten the branches to 1 to 2 leaves. If you want the tree to bloom and produce fruit, do not cut the shoots after the buds appear. Real flowering, however, does not happen for many years.

Wiring: It is best to wire during the main growing season, but only lignified branches.

Propagation: Use either cuttings, seeds, or air layering. The easiest way is with seed. Put the seed in a pot 2 inches (5 cm) wide, and cover with bonsai soil just deep enough so that the seed is not visible. Keep the soil moist. A new little plant will reach for the light after about 10 days.

Ulmus parvifolia
Chinese elm
Family: Ulmaceae
Subtropics

Ulmus parvifolia
Chinese elm

In Asia, this tree grows up to 65 feet tall (20 m). If it is grown in a cool location, it will shed its leaves in the winter. The elm has small, dark green, alternate, dentate leaves attached to the shoots without petioles. Greenish flowers appear in the fall. The crown opens up at the top with slightly trailing branches. The elm is one of the most well-loved as well as the most undemanding of miniature trees. It has been cultivated in China and Taiwan for hundreds of years, charming everybody with its tiny leaves, delicate branching, and its robust, strong trunk. This tree will tolerate all kinds of mistakes, such as overwatering, underwatering, or temperature changes. It is highly recommended as a bonsai for the beginner.

Location: Indoors at a bright, sunny window or, in spring after danger of frost is over, outdoors in a sunny spot. Before the first frost, bring the tree back to its indoor location, where it will do well during the winter months at temperatures ranging from 42 to 71°F (6 to 22°C). If kept in a warm location, the tree needs lots of light and fresh air. If that is not possible, the plant may be subject to red spider mite infestation.

Watering: Allow the soil to become partially dry before watering; this also is recommended during the winter rest period.

Feeding: Use liquid bonsai fertilizer every two weeks. During the winter months, from fall on, if the plant is in a warm location, use it every four to six weeks. It also is recommended that the plant receive one application of pulverized organic fertilizer, sprinkled on top of the soil in the beginning of summer.

Transplanting: Repot every two years at the beginning of spring; include vigorous root pruning.

Soil: Use either bonsai soil or loam, peat moss, and sand at a ratio of 2:1:1.

Wiring: When the branches are well lignified; however, the elm tree is easily shaped with proper pruning alone.

Pruning: Cut shoots back to 2 to 3 leaves after 8 to 12 leaves have developed on new shoots.

Propagation: The fastest way is with cuttings in summer. They will develop roots in a glass of water.

More Plants for Bonsai Growing

The joy of creating bonsai seems to be infectious. More and more people in Europe and North America are turning to cultivating these little trees from the tropics and subtropics, which seem to feel welcome in our homes. The number and variety of different plants offered commercially is growing from year to year.

On the preceding pages, we introduced you to species that have been proven to work well as bonsai. Of course, we could give you only a small sampling of the many that nature offers. Be adventurous and try something new. Let yourself be inspired by trees and bushes that you come across while on vacation; look in flower shops and nurseries, and be courageous and creative.

On the following pages, you will find additional suggestions for plants that are well-suited for creating bonsai that will be comfortable in your home.

Acacia karroo

Acacia baileyana
Cootamundra wattle

These subtropical and tropical trees have small, feathery leaves and golden yellow, fragrant flowers. In some places they are incorrectly called *golden mimosa*. For bonsai, the *Acacia baileyana* and *Acacia farnesiana* are very well suited; even in the wild, they remain small. The *Acacia baileyana* must be kept cool, 46 to 53°F (8 to 12°C) during the winter months, whereas the *Acacia farnesiana* can acclimate to warmer indoor temperatures. Transplant only every two years; keep evenly moist. Other recommended species are: *A. cavenia*, *A. spectabilis*, *A. verticillata*, and *A. karroo*.

Albizia julibrissin
Silk tree, Mimosa

A deciduous tree with feathery leaves and white to light-pink flowers. It is widely known in the tropics and the subtropics of the near and far east. In Europe, it is found in Ticino (southern Switzerland) and along the Mediterranean sea coast. For this reason, treat it as a coldhouse bonsai.

Araucaria heterophylla (A. excelsa)
Norfolk Island pine

The Norfolk Island pine is one of the most well-known trees from subtropical regions. Growing it as an indoor bonsai is very simple. It tolerates warm temperatures and won't mind dry soil. However, it doesn't like direct sunlight.

Ardisia crenata
Coralberry, spiceberry

This evergreen shrub has whitish flowers and pea-sized red berries. It is very charming as a bonsai, since the berries remain on the plant for many months if the plant is kept in a very bright location and the temperature during the winter months is kept between 59 and 64°F (15 and 18°C). *Ardisia* is not heavily branched.

Argyranthemum frutescens (Chrysanthemum frutescens)
Marguerite, Paris daisy

The delicate marguerite is native to the Canary Islands. In nature, the bush grows to about 20 to 39 inches (50 to 100 cm). Even as an indoor plant, it produces countless daisylike flowers throughout almost the whole year. It is a very beautiful, strong little bush. It has coldhouse requirements: a bright location and cool temperatures during the winter months—about 41 to 53°F (5 to 12°C). Water sparingly.

Bambusa multiplex (B. glaucescens)
Hedge bamboo

These tropical, woody grasses are now also found in northern Europe and in the Mediterranean regions, although they originated in China. As an indoor plant, *Bambusa multiplex* does particularly well. It likes a very bright location, but avoid direct sunlight in the summer. It needs a great deal of water, and, during the winter months, should be kept at about 68 to 71°F (20 to 22°C). New leaves develop at the tips of shoots. If you want a compact plant, you must pull off the new leaves before they unfurl.

Bucida spinosa
Spiny black olive

This delicate tree from Florida and the Caribbean grows into a bonsai almost by itself. Water well; prune roots moderately when transplanting in late winter. Shorten new shoots only a little, by picking them off.

Bursera simaruba
West Indian birch, Gumbo-limbo

This tree, which has a resinous sap, can grow up to 49 feet tall (15 m) in its Caribbean habitat. What is noticeable about this tree is its red-brown trunk, from which the bark peels off like transparent parchment paper. The tree has feathery leaves and greenish yellow flowers. Every part of the plant is fragrant. As an indoor bonsai, it doesn't ask for much, tolerating dry spells and heat well. Cuttings root very quickly in moist soil.

Callistemon
Bottlebrush

There are many different species of *Callistemon*. They are native to Australia, where they grow up to 10 feet tall (3 m). They usually have dark green, leathery leaves. This plant needs much sunlight and fresh air. Water it with softened water and keep it uniformly moist. Cut the shoots back vigorously after the plant has finished blooming. Keep the plant at a temperature of about 42 to 50°F (6 to 10°C) during the winter months; of course, water it less during this time. Bring the plant outside in mid-spring.

Carissa macrocarpa
Natal plum

This evergreen, tropical, small-leafed, thorny bush belongs to the Apocynaceae family. When placed in a bright location, the plant develops fragrant, white and pink flowers and edible, dark-red fruit. Water moderately; keep it warm over the winter months. Transplanting is done only in the fall and winter, with minimal root pruning at the same time.

Cassia marilandica
Wild senna

The *Cassia marilandica* is a plant that has been used by native Americans in many ways for a long time. It has a slightly lignified trunk, small compound leaves, and small yellow flowers. Even in nature, it is not a tall bush. As a bonsai, it tolerates somewhat higher temperatures than, for instance, the *Cassia angustifolia* and other *Cassia* species that are often found planted in flowerpots or tubs in subtropical Mediterranean regions. In temperate regions, they can be raised as coldhouse bonsai.

Chamaecyparis pisifera 'Plumosa,' C. pisifera 'Nana Aurea,' and C. pisifera 'Squarrosa'
Sawara cypress

Most of the false cypresses do well only as outdoor bonsai; the ones mentioned here, however, also thrive indoors and are somewhat more tolerant of higher temperatures if the leaves are sprayed with water often. Never keep these plants close to a heating source! A somewhat cool, bright, and airy location is ideal. Water moderately throughout the year, allowing the soil to become partially dry before each watering.

Cinnamomum camphora
Camphor tree

Camphor trees are native to the tropical and subtropical regions of Asia. They can grow up to 131 feet (40 m) tall and have very large trunks that are covered with a thick, rough bark. The oval-shaped, densely growing, shiny leaves are a bit too large for a bonsai, but they can be reduced in size over time. Camphor trees do best in a bright, moderately warm location.

Citrus microcarpa

For care, see *Fortunella hindsii*, on page 125.

Coffea arabica
Arabian coffee plant

C. robusta
Robusta coffee

The coffee tree—with its evergreen, dark green, shiny leaves and star-shaped, white flowers in the summer and red berries in the fall—will be a charming addition to your collection. During the summer months, keep the plant in a window that is primarily in the shade; do not place it at a southern exposure; in the winter months, keep it in a very bright location. Spray the plant and water it generously and often during its main growing period; during the winter months, depending on the temperature indoors, water sparingly, but don't let the root ball dry out completely. Ideal temperatures for the winter months are between 60 and 71°F (16 and 22°C).

Cotoneaster microphyllus and C. microphyllus 'Cochleatus'

These evergreen plants grow slowly and have small leaves, white flowers, and red berries. When kept in a coldhouse environment, they develop into beautiful bonsai and are also excellent candidates for creating miniature bonsai.

Crassula sarcocaulis

A member of the succulent family, this plant is originally from South Africa. It is easily formed into an umbrella shape, and the bark quickly looks lignified. It needs lots of light and fresh air and should not be cut back from early summer on, if flowering is desired. Vigorous pruning should be done after blooming is over. For care see, *Portulacaria afra*, on page 155.

Cuphea hyssopifolia
False heather

This small branched shrub from Central America has small, narrow leaves and delicate, purple-red flowers; it is very well-suited to be a miniature bonsai. Do not allow the root ball to dry out; always keep the soil somewhat moist. A sunny, warm location is also important.

Cytisus racemosus

The *Cytisus*, or broom, is often used as a hedge. *Cytisus racemosus* produces many yellow flowers and thrives as an indoor bonsai. It requires coldhouse conditions: an airy, bright, cool location during the winter months, with temperatures between 46 and 53°F (8 and 12°C). It likes soil rich in lime.

Diospyros rhodocalyx
Persimmon, Date plum

This tropical evergreen tree has pitch-black, rough bark and loves to grow beneath other tall trees. There are almost 200 species of *Diospyros*. Its leaves are almost round. This tree does not look very appealing during its dormant period; however, it becomes more appealing when new growth begins in the spring. It is important to provide good drainage and high humidity for the plant. Keep temperatures around 64°F (18°C) during the winter. Leaf pruning in early summer is helpful in keeping the leaves small. Be sure to water moderately.

Eucalyptus citriodora
Lemon-scented gum

E. ficifolia
Red-flowering gum

E. gunnii
Cider gum

E. rhodantha
Rose mallee

All of these fast-growing trees are at home in the subtropical climate zones and belong to the Myrtaceae family. The temperatures during the winter months should be from 53 to 64°F (12 to 18°C). Bring the plant outside during the summer months and place it in full sunlight. Keep it uniformly moist, and do not allow the root ball to dry out. Cut shoots back to one or two leaves. It is not all that easy to transform this plant into a bonsai, because it is difficult to keep it for a long period of time in the same container.

Eugenia brasiliensis
Brazil cherry

This evergreen ornamental shrub has shiny green leaves, new shoots that are red, and white flowers on panicles. Good light conditions are necessary for the tree to develop its deep red, edible fruit. Like all myrtle plants, the *Eugenia brasiliensis* prefers a slightly acid soil, but it is able to tolerate considerably higher temperatures (64 to 68°F [18 to 20°C]) than its relatives.

Eurya japonica

The *Eurya japonica* is an evergreen, decorative shrub from Japan with leathery, dark green leaves, small flowers, and ball-shaped, black berries. It needs to be kept warm during the winter months, and the soil should always be moist.

Eugenia uniflora
Surinam cherry, Brazil cherry

Also called *pitanga*, this *Eugenia* is native to tropical America. It has solitary white flowers and edible, round, yellow to brilliant red fruit that have longitudinal grooves. The leaves are ovate, smooth, and dark green; its new shoots are fiery red. For care, see *Eugenia myrtifolia*, on page 107.

Euonymus japonica 'Variegata'
Japanese spindle tree

This slow-growing evergreen tree, with its multicolored leaves, will tolerate indoor conditions up to a point. During the winter months, keep the plant in a bright location at temperatures of about 46 to 59°F (8 to 15°C), although a somewhat warmer spot is also acceptable. During the summer, bring the plant outside, to a balcony, terrace, or garden, but return it inside in the fall. Propagate with cuttings.

Euphorbia balsamifera

Originally from the Canary Islands (Tenerife), this plant reaches about 3 feet (1 m) in height. Its natural shape can be altered by pruning branches and twigs that interfere with the desired final form. This plant needs lots of light and little water in order to thrive. Temperatures during the winter months should be around 46 to 60°F (8 to 16°C); outside, the plant loves exposure to full sunlight.

Ficus virens
Spotted fig

For care, see *Ficus religiosa*, on page 121.

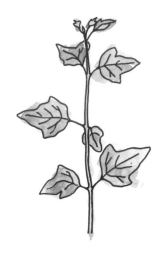

Gmelina hystrix
Hedgehog bush

This climbing, tropical plant belongs to the Verbenaceae family; it is very similar in its habits to the *Bougainvillea*. The ivylike, dark-green leaves are dull on the surface. Its flowers are yellow, and its bracts are purplish red. The plant comes from the Philippines, and it needs little water, a bright location, but not direct sunlight. Usually the thin shoots grow out from a thick root stock, which makes this plant a very interesting choice for a small indoor forest.

Guaiacum officinale
Lignum-vitae

This dense Caribbean evergreen tree has a grayish white, very conspicuous bark. Even as a bonsai, it will develop flowers of an intense blue color if kept in a place with moderate light. Keep the plant warm during the winter months. Shaping and forming the tree is best done by means of cutting and pruning, because the branches are very hard and not very pliable. Let the soil dry partially before each watering.

Grevillea rosmarinifolia

The *Grevillea rosmarinifolia* is very similar to the rosemary bush with its needlelike little leaves. It has bright red flowers that grow in clusters. During the winter months, the plant needs a cool spot—a spot that is light, but not near a heating source. During the summer, it thrives outdoors. The *Grevillea* needs much light and fresh air. Water generously during the growth period, and sparingly during the winter months, but do not let the soil become completely dry.

Hedera helix
English ivy

English ivy is a robust plant that tolerates a dark location as well as a bright one. However, it takes time for the branches to thicken and take on the character of a tree.

Hibiscus rosa-sinensis
Chinese hibiscus

In the subtropics, the *Hibiscus rosa-sinensis* grows as a small tree. In other regions, it is well-loved as an evergreen houseplant. It has shiny green leaves and large, funnel-shaped, pinkish red flowers. Temperatures during the winter months should be between 53 and 59°F (12 and 15°C); water generously during the main growing period and when the plant is in bloom. It is easy to transform the Chinese hibiscus into a bonsai.

Hibiscus tiliaceus
Mahoe

This evergreen tree can be kept quite warm during the winter months. A very bright location is important for the development of its leaves and flowers. Allow the soil to become partially dry before watering. The *Hibiscus tiliaceus* benefits much from vigorous pruning.

Ilex asprella

In Taiwan, this deciduous holly tree grows in forests under larger trees. It has black bark with tiny white dots and alternate leaves that have dark green veins. Small white flowers appear simultaneously with the leaves in the spring and later produce small, egg-shaped, black, pea-sized fruit. Its branches naturally grow horizontally, towards the outside. The plant tolerates full sunlight as well as partial shade. Water moderately. The ideal location is a place whose temperature range is 59 to 64°F (15 to 18°C). Cutting leaves in early summer does not present a problem.

Ilex crenata, Ilex crenata 'Mariesii'
Japanese holly

Both of these holly trees have small leaves. Shaping them into a bonsai is best accomplished by pruning rather than wiring, because their branches are very brittle. The female *Ilex vomitoria* (yaupow) develops red berries when the flowers have been pollinated.

Ixora javanica

With its fiery red flowers, the *Ixora javanica* is one of the most magnificent ornamental shrubs of the tropics. When cultivated as an indoor bonsai, it needs slightly acidic soil. The plant will do well even in low light, but it will flower only when kept at a very bright window, with temperatures throughout the year around 64 to 71°F (18 to 22°C).

Leptospermum scoparium
New Zealand tea tree

A member of the Myrtaceae family, this plant is an ornamental shrub from New Zealand with thorn-tipped, lanceolate leaves and small, white, roselike flowers. It needs to be in a bright, cool location and uniformly moist; its roots should be pruned only very lightly. The New Zealand tea tree needs a lot of fresh air; do not keep it near a heat source.

Ligustrum lucidum Ligustrum japonicum rotundifolium
Glossy privet Wax-leaf privet

Both of these Asiatic evergreen privets do well as indoor bonsai because of their beautiful shiny green leaves. The *Ligustrum lucidum* (glossy privet) has magnificent flowers. Both species like a cool location during the winter months, but will adapt to warmer conditions.

Myrsine africana
Cape myrtle, African boxwood

This small, dense bush, whose habitat is South Africa, has small dark green leaves, inconspicuous reddish brown flowers, and blue berries. It is a dioecious plant, which means that, if you want fruit, you must have two plants: a female and a male, as the staminate and pistillate flowers are on separate plants. Wiring is essential if you want to give this tree some elegance, because the branches are very stiff and straight. The care is the same for the *Myrtis communis* (see page 147).

Nandina domestica
Heavenly bamboo, Sacred bamboo

A member of the Berberidaceae family, this plant originated in Asia. It is a very interesting plant: Its new shoots are pink, and it develops yellow to dark green leaves, which turn red in the fall. Also, in the fall, the plant produces red berries. But it is not all that easy to grow as a bonsai; it is difficult to shape it into a good form. Bring the plant outside during the summer. During the winter keep it inside, in a winter garden, between 50 and 60°F (10 and 16°C), watering sparingly. The *Nandina* will shed its leaves if it is kept in a warmer location, but they will grow again in the spring.

Nicodemia (Buddleia) diversifolia
Butterfly bush

This is an ornamental bush whose native habitat is Madagascar. It has wavy, lobate leaves with pronounced veins, which can slowly be reduced to the desired bonsai size. The tree can be shaped exclusively by pruning. During the winter, keep it in a bright location, with temperatures between 50 and 71°F (10 and 22°C). When indoors, it needs lots of water and will tolerate a location with less light. Propagation is done with cuttings.

Ochna serrulata
Bird's-eye bush, Mickey-Mouse plant

This subtropical shrub, whose home is in South Africa, tends to grow unwieldy; for this reason, to achieve an elegant form, begin shaping the bonsai while the plant is still young. Its bright yellow sepals are particularly charming. The black fruit is suspended from the calyx, which has in the meantime changed to a brilliant red. The plant needs to be repotted every two years. It should be kept outdoors in the spring and cool during the winter months, with sufficient light. The soil needs to be kept uniformly moist. The *Ochna kirkii*, whose home is in the tropical regions of Africa, should be kept in a somewhat warmer location in winter.

Pelargonium rhodanthum
Geranium

Of the many *Pelargonium* species—commonly known as *Geranium*—this plant works particularly well as a bonsai, since it remains small and has small heart- or kidney-shaped greyish green leaves and pink to deep red flowers. The *Pelargonium* likes a bright location and should be watered sparingly. It will shed its leaves if kept too wet. Temperatures during the winter months should be about 60°F (16°C). *Pelargonium* need much fresh air and light.

Pemphis acidula
Silver willow

This evergreen tree, which will tolerate saline soil, has small, silver-grey, opposite leaves and white flowers. The bark, depending on the variety, can be either rough or smooth, and is light grey. All varieties need to be watered generously and need sufficient amounts of fertilizer. Keep the plant in a warm location during the winter months, with temperatures not below 60°F (16°C). This plant is relatively difficult to grow in cool regions.

Phylica ericoides

A delicate evergreen plant, similar to heather, with small, needle-shaped leaves and white flowers in fascicles, it makes a beautiful bonsai when kept in a coldhouse. Place the plant in a bright, sunny location. Water moderately, letting the soil dry out partially; use softened water.

Pinus halepensis
Aleppo pine, Jerusalem pine

Pinus pinea
Italian stone pine

These seem to be the only pine trees that will do well indoors, provided that, during the winter months, they can be kept in a cool location (41 to 50°F [5 to 10°C]). Bring these plants outside from mid spring through summer, and place them in the full sun. Water sparingly. Wiring should be done during the winter months. New shoots should be shortened by a third with your fingers before they open up. Old needles dry from the inside out and should be removed, because they don't fall off by themselves.

Pithecellobium dulce
Manila tamarind

This is a fast-growing tree with a wide crown. The featherlike leaves are grey-green and fold together in the wind and at dusk. The flowers are yellowish white, and the fruit is reddish. The plant needs a lot of light, temperatures between 59 and 71°F (15 and 22°C), and sandy soil. Keep the soil moderately moist during the summer, and during the winter allow the root ball to dry out partially before watering again. Cut new shoots back to two to three pairs of leaves after they have developed 10 to 12 pairs of leaves.

Pittosporum tobira
Japanese *Pittosporum*

A dense, subtropical evergreen tree with leatherlike, shiny, dark green leaves, producing very fragrant flowers in spring. As a bonsai, the plant should be kept in a bright, cool location and receive the same care as the myrtle plants.

Pyracantha
Fire thorn

Species like *P. angustifolia* and *P. crenatoserrata*, evergreen plants often used as hedges, also make very decorative bonsai, with their small leaves, white flowers in the spring, and red berries in the fall. They like to be in a cool location during the winter and need to be watered generously when in bloom and when the fruit ripens; otherwise, water moderately. *P. koidzumii* can be kept in a slightly warmer location.

Quercus suber
Cork oak

The cork oak is an evergreen tree with a gnarled trunk. It is native to the Mediterranean region and highly recommended as a bonsai. It needs a coldhouse climate; water moderately and transplant every 2 to 3 years. The tree needs very little root pruning. If you want to collect these trees, choose only very young trees, because older ones don't tolerate root pruning very well.

Raphiolepis indica
Indian hawthorn

The Indian hawthorn is a very decorative, low- and slow-growing ornamental bush, with leathery leaves, pinkish white flowers, and blue-black fruit. The bonsai is shaped only by means of pruning, because its brittle branches are difficult to wire. A coldhouse location is best, but the plant can adapt to warmer temperatures.

Sophora prostrata

The *Sophora prostrata* is a prostrate or ascending shrub, which grows very slowly in its native New Zealand. It sheds most of its leaves in winter. *Sophora* needs a lot of light and fresh air. During the winter months, keep it in a cool location and water it sparingly.

Taxodium distichum
Bald cypress

The bald cypress is a deciduous conifer, and it makes a very decorative indoor bonsai. This plant likes to be kept cool and dry during the winter months; it loses its needles during this time. It needs plentiful water and a bright, airy location in the spring, at the beginning of the active growing period.

Trachelospermum jasminoides
Star jasmine

The star jasmine is an evergreen tree with elliptical, leathery leaves and strongly scented white flowers in panicles. It makes a beautiful bonsai, which thrives in coldhouse conditions.

Triphasia trifolia
Limeberry

This is a slow-growing citrus plant with small white flowers (similar to those of the *Murraya*) and small, round, dark red fruit the size of a fingernail. As a bonsai, it does well in partial shade with plenty of fertilizer, sandy soil, and not too much water. It needs a bright location, but should not be exposed to direct sunlight. During the winter months, it should be kept at temperatures below 59°F (15°C). A spot outdoors for the summer does it a world of good.

Vitex agnus-castus
Chaste tree, Monk's pepper tree

This is a small tree—13 feet tall (4 m)—with light blue flowers in the fall. The bark has a wonderful beige color, and the trunk is strong. This plant has been cultivated as a bonsai in Thailand for a long time. It needs a large amount of light and fresh air; too little light causes a loss of leaves. This plant sometimes is difficult to grow indoors; however, it can be grown successfully in a winter garden. The plant does best outdoors from mid spring through summer. Keep it in the winter garden for the winter months, at temperatures between 53 and 59°F (12 and 15°C). During the dormant period, it usually sheds its leaves, but they grow again in the spring. During the dormant period, water sparingly; during the summer months, let the soil dry partially before watering again.

Wrightia
or Holarrhena antidysenterica

A tropical, evergreen shrub with small branches and decorative, fuchsialike, white flowers. It should be shaped into the desired bonsai form when the plant is still young. Keep temperatures during the winter months between 64 and 68°F (18 and 20°C). This little tree loves high humidity and needs much light. It should be watered generously during its long flowering period.

Outdoor Bonsai That Can Be Grown Indoors

Sometimes it is just an accident—sometimes the result of boldness—but time and again the amateur gardener has had experiences that defy everything that has been discussed so far.

Nature won't be ruled by people. This is the reason that bonsai that we think will only thrive outdoors often have been kept indoors successfully for years. If the gardener is asked what kind of special care is given, the answer is: the two most important ingredients are sufficient light and air. Trees and bushes, whose natural environment is the outdoors, should be protected from temperatures that are too high, which means not placing your plants near or above a heat source, so that they can have the necessary dormant period. If outdoor bonsai are to thrive inside, they must be kept in a cool, bright, and airy location and receive very careful attention.

Here are a few outdoor genera that gardeners have successfully grown indoors: fire thorn (*Pyracantha*), juniper, cypress, *Zelkova*, false cypress, *Cotoneaster*, *Ginkgo*, and *Thuja*.

Pyracantha

Answers to Important Questions

Learn by asking questions.

Good Advice from Bonsai Specialists

1. Do indoor bonsai thrive exclusively indoors?

No, because our living quarters are not the natural environment for plants. Certain subtropical and tropical plants do grow well indoors—particularly in a coldhouse environment—but they love to be outside during the summer months, in a location protected from the wind. Check the suggestions given for specific plants on pages 87–173.

2. Is it possible to bring outdoor bonsai inside?

For a short period of time, yes. For instance, for special occasions when you want to use the plant as decoration. This does not present a problem during the summer, when temperature differences between the indoors and the outdoors are negligible. However, if you want to bring a plant indoors during the winter months, make sure that it is not near or above a heat source. It is also important for the bonsai to have sufficient light.

3. Can an indoor bonsai be shaped and transplanted any time during the year?

Generally speaking, yes. The optimal time, however, is right before the plants begin their active growing period in spring. Plants in bloom are transplanted after the flowering period.

4. How often should I shorten/prune/cut new shoots?

When they have become slightly lignified, or when they have developed about six to eight pairs of leaves.

5. How often should I transplant an indoor bonsai?

This depends on the species and age of your bonsai. Young, fast-growing plants should be transplanted every year; older and slower growing plants should be transplanted every two to three years.

6. Isn't root pruning a "painful" intrusion in the natural development of a plant?

No. The removal of dead roots protects the plant from rot and decay. Shortening the roots by a third encourages root growth and fosters healthy development. Both are only done when you are repotting the plant or when the root ball has become too dense.

7. Many negative opinions prevail regarding the wiring of branches and twigs. Are they justified?

No. Proper and careful wiring does not injure a plant, but makes it more beautiful. Such shaping is a much more gentle process than the many influences a tree has to endure in nature, such as storms, hail, and rock slides.

8. At what point does a gardener decide which form to choose for a bonsai plant?

In peace and quiet, the gardener will look "into" the shape of the growing plant in order to detect the form that nature gave it. Such contemplation gives the gardener the necessary insight as well as an understanding of which of the classic bonsai forms is the most appropriate.

9. Is there such a thing as a "bonsai seed"?

No, even if the description on some seed packages seems to imply it. The description on these packages should really read: "seeds suitable for bonsai."

10. **What is a solitaire?**

A particularly beautifully shaped tree that is at least 25 years old.

11. **Which plants are recommended for the beginner?**

Always begin with young plants. All rubber trees (*Ficus*) work well, since they thrive indoors without any problems. In addition, the elm and the cherry bush are good for beginners, because they are very forgiving when it comes to mistakes.

12. **What is the life expectancy of an indoor bonsai?**

There are no hard and fast rules. Particularly in their native habitat, but even in other regions, we know of bonsai trees that are 100 years old. However, like everything else in nature, bonsai are subject to the laws that govern living and dying. Some live only a relatively short time.

13. **What has happened to a bonsai when it gets sick?**

One possibility may have to do with the plant's location. Even if it is placed close to a window, it may need additional (artificial) light. Or, often the humidity is too low. Are you watering properly? Too much watering is as bad as too little. When in doubt, read the part of the chapter about diseases and pests. If you still cannot determine the reason for your problem, check with an expert at a nursery or botanical garden.

14. **Is there a rule of thumb for watering?**

The following will always work: don't let the soil dry out completely. Following this advice, let the surface of the soil become slightly dry and then water carefully. Better yet, immerse the plant—in its container—in a water bath.

15. Is spraying the plant the way to increase humidity?

It is not the best method. Trays or containers filled with water, a water garden, or a water fountain are more effective.

16. What is the cause of the white deposits sometimes seen at the base of a trunk and the edge of the container?

Hard water, containing too much lime. While these deposits are not harmful, they are unsightly. They can be prevented by using soft water for watering.

17. Are "wet feet" dangerous for bonsai?

They are certainly not healthy. Excess water remaining in the saucer should be emptied.

18. Can there be good or even beneficial animals in bonsai?

Yes, just as in the earth outdoors. Think, for instance, of earthworms and snails. . . . Remember, wherever there is earth, there is life. Allow it to be (unless it is a destructive pest).

19. Do indoor bonsai need to be fed?

Yes, just like other plants. See the index regarding fertilizers, or individual species instructions.

20. Should I feed a sick plant?

No. Weakened plants can only take up small amounts of nutrition. Additional fertilizer would damage the plant even further.

21. Is a tree sick if it loses all or part of its green leaves? (a special problem for *Ficus* trees)

Not necessarily. The most common reason is improper care: too little light and "cold" or "wet feet."

22. What is happening when the leaves turn yellow at the inside of the tree?

This is usually nothing to worry about. It may be part of a normal process whereby older leaves are replaced to make room for new leaves; or else, the tree may not have enough light and air inside the crown. The tree may be suffering from a temporary drought. As long as the tree produces new shoots and leaves, everything is in order.

23. Why does moss last such a short time indoors?

Indoor bonsai usually come from a greenhouse. While the tree itself thrives, the surrounding moss does not. It is normal for the moss to become brown after a short time; this is not an indication that mistakes in care have been made.

24. How does one lose the fear of pruning or cutting?

Think of your hair: the more it is cut, the faster it grows. The same holds true for plants. Cutting back shoots and twigs encourages new growth.

25. Are bonsai appropriate for the office and a 5-day week?

Absolutely. Water the bonsai—using the immersion method— and no harm will come over the weekend.

26. Why are bonsai so much more expensive than other houseplants?

From the many plants available to us, only a limited number can be transformed into bonsai. In addition, every tree represents an enormous investment in time, gardening know-how, and creativity.

27. Is the age of a bonsai plant important in terms of its value?

Age is only one criterion in determining the value of these small trees. Just as important is their form. Of course, many particularly beautiful specimens can be found among older trees—but younger trees can also be very charming and beautiful.

28. How does one counter those critics who insist it is not right to force a tree to remain small?

Here is one answer: As is the case with human beings, plants too differ genetically, each one having very distinct developmental possibilities. Depending on where a plant lives it will develop a certain way. In rich soil and in a good climate, a plant will grow faster and become larger. If the soil is poor, or if it grows on a rock ledge or a high elevation with a short growing season and often harsh winds, a plant will grow more slowly and remain smaller. Both situations already are present in nature.

Buying Indoor Bonsai

Beauty is in the eyes of the beholder.

How to Avoid Paying for Mistakes

If we ask an experienced bonsai gardener, who has collected and nurtured many particularly beautiful bonsai over a span of many years, about the criteria for determining the quality of a bonsai plant, we will hear answers like: "The most important factor in determining the value of a small bonsai tree is its natural beauty" and: "You recognize a master of the perfectly cultivated tree; the person was able to visualize its natural beauty."

But in spite of such vague statements, let's try to describe the characteristics that make a bonsai plant valuable. Regardless of whether it is a formal upright, windswept, or cascade form, the shape of a tree should be clean and definite. Another sign of quality is that the trunk is somewhat wider at the base, tapering as it reaches the crown. This conveys the impression of a strong, well-rooted plant. The crown is considered aesthetically pleasing if the tree has branched out well, giving it a distinctly defined form.

A small tree is always valuable if it is obvious that it has grown harmoniously into its own form. If the form of a tree has impressed you and you can easily remember it, then it is most likely a good choice. The "personality" of a bonsai, therefore, is more important than its age. A young tree with a well-balanced shape whose trunk, branches, twigs, and leaves (or needles) are in harmony may be more valuable than an older tree whose form looks artificial and complicated.

Very often a bonsai that has character shows visible evidence of cutting. Such evidence is not considered to diminish a plant's quality and value. On the contrary: well-healed cuts and "beautiful scars" are evidence of the expertise and love the bonsai gardener has employed; they add to the personality and dignity of the bonsai plant.

Of course, a bonsai must be healthy. The amateur gardener will judge a plant's health by determining how strong it looks and how

Top: Vitex agnus-castus, distinctly and simply shaped. Bottom: Ficus religiosa with very beautiful offshoots from the trunk.

The tree and container form a unit.

fresh its leaves are. However, even experienced bonsai gardeners will tell you, time and again, that buying a bonsai plant is a matter of having faith in the people who sell them, because you cannot look "inside" a tree. We recommended, therefore, buying from a specialist who is also able to give advice on care and other aspects of bonsai-raising, and who guarantees the quality of the plant. Such criteria are much more important than going where the price is lower.

Buying from mail-order houses has become an interesting development of late. It surely is a function of the improvements that the packaging industry has made that today we, almost as a matter of course, trust that the postal service can ship our plants safely. And, indeed, they do arrive unharmed and healthy. This accounts for the fact that more and more bonsai plants are selected in the comfort of our home.

Trees that have been grown by experts can also be recognized by their containers. The plant and container should visually complement each other, looking as if they belong together naturally. If a container is too big the plant might look like it is drowning; when a container seems to be too small, it will look as if the plant is about to tip over.

With containers, as well, practice makes perfect. Once you start looking at the whole—becoming alert to the proper proportion between the plant and the container—you will be able to judge whether the bonsai was created by an expert.

Just as with any other hobby, many different ways are available for the bonsai enthusiast to gain knowledge; for example, getting to know a master, participating in seminars, and joining bonsai clubs. Your nearest botanical garden may be able to help you find the one nearest to you.

Index

---

*Asterisk indicates an illustration.

Photo Sources and Contributors

Artemis-Verlag, Munich and Zürich
Peter Bloomer, Florida, US
Günter Blum, Fotodesign, Heidelberg, Germany
Helmut Brenner, Aichtal, Germany
Achim Bunz, Windach, Germany
Kora E. Daiager, San Diego, US
Udo Fischer, Bammental, Germany
C. Franchi, Pescia, Italy
Eberhard Grames, Germany
Antonio Gravalos Esteban, Spain
Te Chang Huang, Taiwan
Iberbonsai S.A., Alboraya/Valencia, Spain
Saburo Kato, Japan
Peter Krebs, Herborn, Germany
Ilona Lesniewicz, Heidelberg, Germany
Wu Ma, Taiwan
Mary Madison, Homestead, Florida, US
Juan Antonio Montijano, Spain
Felipe Recio Moreno, Spain
John Naka, California, US
Jyoti & Nikunj Parekh, Bombay, India
Arthur Rammacher, Hanau, Germany
Ana Saenz-Pisaca, Santa Cruz de Tenerife, Spain
Lothar Schattat, Santa Cruz de Tenerife, Spain
SIHEMA, Mannheim, Germany
James Smith, Vero Beach, Florida, US
Tony + Bubpa T. Tanakul, Bangkok, Thailand
Amparo Vieco, Spain
Huang Jiu Wei, Canton, China
Josef Wiegand, Heidelberg, Germany